Accompaniment on Theorbo
and Harpsichord

Publications of the Early Music Institute
Thomas Binkley, General Editor

Accompaniment on Theorbo and Harpsichord
Denis Delair's Treatise of 1690

A TRANSLATION WITH COMMENTARY

by

Charlotte Mattax

INDIANA UNIVERSITY PRESS
Bloomington & Indianapolis

Manufactured in the United States of America

Library of Congress Cataloguing-in-Publication Data

Delair, Denis.
    [*Traité d'accompagnement pour le théorbe et le clavecin.* English]
    Accompaniment on theorbo and harpsichord: Denis Delair's treatise of 1690 / a
translation with commentary by Charlotte Mattax.
    p.   cm. -- (Publications of the Early Music Institute)
    Translation of: *Traité d'accompagnement pour le théorbe et le clavecin.*
    Includes bibliographical references and index.
    ISBN 0-253-28592-5 (pbk.)
    1. Musical accompaniment--Early works to 1800. 2. Thorough bass--Early
       works to 1800. 3. Theorbo--Methods--Early works to 1800. 4. Harpsichord--
       Methods--Early works to 1800. I. Mattax, Charlotte. II. Title. III. Series.
MT68.D4413 1991
786.4'147--dc20
                                          90-49917

1 2 3 4 5 95 94 93 92 91

For My Family

and

Friends

Contents

Facsimiles

Acknowledgments

It is with great pleasure that I acknowledge the influence and support of a number of professors at Stanford University, where I began this project. I am indebted to Dr. George Houle for his encouragement and guidance, to Dr. Albert Cohen for his meticulous attention to detail and useful conversation about French theory, and to Dr. Marc Bertrand for his reading of the French translation. Gratitude is extended to Dr. Robert Darnton, of Princeton University, for his advice on 18th-century French biographical research, and to Dr. Richard Chrisman, of Rutgers University, for his insight on theoretical aspects of Delair's treatise. I wish also to express appreciation to Éditions Minkoff and Kluwer Academic Publishers for permitting the reproduction of facsimiles from their editions of the treatises of Delair and Mersenne, and to Apple Music Copy Services for preparing the remaining musical examples. Finally, my thanks go to the reference librarians of Rutgers, Princeton and Stanford Universities, and the staff of both the Bibliothèque de la Ville de Paris and the Archives Nationales in Paris, France, for their assistance in locating materials.

Notes on the Translation

   This translation is based on the Minkoff reprint of the 1690 edition of Delair's *Traité d'accompagnement pour le théorbe, et le clavecin.* The original is located in Paris at the Bibliothèque Nationale (Vm 8-u 5, 6). The additions and corrections made by Delair in the *Nouveau traité* of 1724 (B.N. Vm 8-u 7) have been incorporated into the translation of the 1690 edition, and have been footnoted where they occur. The revised edition contains two new sections--"General Rules" and an "Addendum"-- which have been included in their entirety. Due to the nature of the prose, I have sometimes translated freely to get to the essence of the meaning, but only when absolutely necessary. Any changes from the original text have been bracketed. The translation of some terms presented special problems. A discussion of these terms and the equivalents I have elected to use in English can be found in the Glossary. The examples Delair gives to illustrate his text have been numbered to facilitate study. Revisions to these examples have been bracketed. Page numbers referenced in footnotes are those of the original *Traité*. They can be found in brackets at the right of the corresponding page in the translation.

Translator's Commentary

Significance

Denis Delair's *Traité d'accompagnement pour le théorbe, et le clavecin*,[1] published in Paris in 1690, is one of the earliest French manuals on basso continuo accompaniment. Although preceded by others, including Nicolas Fleury, Angelo Michele Bartolotti and Guillaume-Gabriel Nivers,[2] Delair claims to be the first to discuss accompaniment thoroughly:

> . . . no one, up to the present, has treated the subject of accompaniment in depth, either because there are few people who wish to take the trouble to learn all the rules necessary to accompany perfectly, or because most have learned to accompany by rote, and teach it in the same way.[3]

---

[1]Denis Delair, *Traité d'accompagnement pour le théorbe, et le clavecin* (Paris: l'auteur, 1690. Facs. ed. Geneva: Minkoff, 1972).

[2]Nicolas Fleury, *Méthode pour apprendre facilement à toucher le théorbe sur la basse continue* (Paris: Ballard, 1660). Facs. ed. Geneva: Minkoff, 1972; Angelo Michele Bartolotti (Bartolomi), *Table pour apprendre à toucher le théorbe sur la basse continue* (Paris: Ballard, 1669); Guillaume-Gabriel Nivers, "L'Art d'accompagner sur la basse continue," *Motets à voix seule accompagnée de la basse-continue* (Paris: l'auteur, 1689). Trans. by William Pruitt, "The Organ Works of G.-G. Nivers (1631-1714)," *Recherches sur la musique française classique* (Paris: Editions A. & J. Picard, 1974), vol. 14, pp. 38-42. Partial trans. with commentary by Madeleine Garros, "L'Art d'accompagner sur la basse-continue d'après Guillaume-Gabriel Nivers," *Mélanges d'histoire et d'esthéthique musicales offerts à Paul Marie Masson*, 2 vols. (Paris: Richard Masse, ed., 1955), vol. 2, pp. 45-51.

[3]Delair, *Traité*, p. [A] (Mattax, p. 41).

Delair's *Traité* appears to have been a respected and well-known method in its time, yet its significance has been largely overlooked in the present day. As a guide to French thoroughbass accompaniment, the book offers practical advice of particular value to harpsichord and theorbo players, with remarks on voice leading, the completion of chords over partially figured and unfigured basses, and the style of continuo playing.

In the *Traité*, Delair describes a rich accompaniment, embellished by means of freely arpeggiated chords and *coulés* in the tradition of the *prélude nonmesuré*.[4] In the revised edition of 1724, the *Nouveau traité*, he shows how to enliven a thinly textured continuo part by metrically breaking the notes of the chord. According to Delair, these examples illustrate the different textures suitable for slow and fast movements. At the same time, they parallel a change in style from the elaborate writing of seventeenth-century *clavecinistes* to the *style galant* of eighteenth-century composers.[5]

Similarly, with a thirty-four year time span bridging two centuries, the first and second editions provide the student of French theory with information about the transition from modality to tonality and the increasing use of chromaticism by French composers in the eighteenth century. Delair is progressive in including augmented and diminished chords and is forward-looking in some of his realizations of diatonic chords as well. One of the first French writers to mention the double sharp,[6] he is at the forefront of seventeenth-century French theory in setting forth the concept of enharmonic equivalence.

Throughout the *Traité*, Delair writes for the performer. He stresses the importance of acquiring facility before subtlety in continuo playing. The intricate counterpoint a composer might write may not be readily improvised by the accompanist who, Delair observes, "is obliged to play, on the spot, appropriate chords which a composer would have notated only with a good deal of time, trouble and travail."[7] To this end, Delair devises several innovative study aids, among them a table of figured-bass signatures and a system of chord classification. In order to simplify the task of the harpsichordist in learning to decipher complex figures, he reduces the number of chords to four, by grouping together those chords which share the same right-hand accompaniment.

---

[4]See Arlette Zenatti, "La prélude dans la musique profane de clavier en France, au XVIIIe siècle," *Rercherches sur la musique française classique*, vol. 5 (1965), p. 179.

[5]The importance of this change in style is noted in the "Translator's Introduction" to *Principles of the Harpsichord by Monsieur de Saint Lambert* (Paris, 1702), translated and edited by Rebecca Harris-Warrick (Cambridge: Cambridge University Press, 1984), p. vii.

[6]Gene Henry Anderson, *Musical Terminology in J.-P. Rameau's "Traité de l'harmonie": A Study and Glossary Based on an Index*, Ph.D. Diss., University of Iowa, 1981. (Ann Arbor: University Microfilms, 1984), p. 95.

[7]Delair, *Traité*, p. [A] (Mattax, p. 41).

Although Delair's modification of the chord classification system arose primarily as a solution to the problem of interpreting complicated figures, its importance to the development of the concept of triadic inversion should not be dismissed. Monsieur de Saint Lambert copied Delair's idea; moreover, it is entirely possible that Jean-Philippe Rameau took the concept as a starting point for his theory of chord inversion.[8]

The *Traité* as Viewed by Delair's Contemporaries

Rameau himself gives singular praise to Delair. In his *Dissertation sur les différentes méthodes d'accompagnement pour le clavecin, ou l'orgue* (Paris, 1732), Rameau maintains that no other writer deserves more respect: " . . . of all the authors who have undertaken to give us rules for accompaniment, none seems to merit more regard than this one [Delair]. . . ."[9] Furthermore, he applauds Delair's progressiveness: "We are . . . obligated to this author for his research; we were not as advanced until [Delair], and can only profit from [his work]."[10]

From Rameau's comments concerning Delair's second edition, entitled *Nouveau traité d'accompagnement* (Paris, 1724),[11] we can infer that the pamphlet enjoyed wide circulation. The new edition is taken from the same plates as the first. The most significant difference, aside from a few small changes to the original text, is the addition of eighteen pages. In these extra pages, Delair discusses the enrichment of the accompaniment with dissonances, *points d'orgue*, the importance of tonic and dominant relationships in recognizing keys, and the realization of unfigured basses by means of the *rule of the octave*. Rameau asserts that, although François Campion was one of the first to promote this rule,[12] it was not

---

[8]James Burchill, *Saint Lambert's "Nouveau traité de l'accompagnement:"* a *Translation with Commentary*, Ph.D. diss., University of Rochester, 1979 (Ann Arbor: University Microfilms, 1979), p. 122.

[9]" . . . de tous les Auteurs qui ont entrepris de nous donner des Règles d'Accompagnement, il n'y en a point qui semble mériter plus d'egard que celui-ci [Delair]." Jean-Philippe Rameau, *Dissertation sur les différentes méthodes d'accompagnement pour le clavecin, ou pour l'orgue* (Paris, 1732), p. 5.

[10]"Nous avons . . . obligation . . . à ses recherches, on n'avoit pas encore été si avant jusqu'à lui. . . ." Rameau, *Dissertation*, p. 7.

[11]Delair, *Nouveau traité d'accompagnment pour le théorbe, et le clavecin* (Paris: l'auteur et Boivin, 1724).

[12]François Campion, *Traité d'accompagnement et de composition, selon la règle des octaves de musique* (Paris, 1716. Facs. ed. Geneva: Minkoff, 1976). In fact, the *regola dell'ottava* was already known in Italy by this time. Francesco Gasparini published a version of the rule in *l'Armonico pratico al cimbalo* (Venice, 1708; later edns. Venice, 1715, 1729, 1745, 1764, 1802, and Bologna, 1713, 1722). Trans. by Frank S. Stillings as *The Practical*

until Delair included it in the 1724 revision that its use became common practice in France:

> The *Rule of the Octave*, a rule almost generally accepted
> . . . did not this rule take root in France only after the
> [second] edition of this treatise?[13]

The dates of publication of the first and second editions are not in question; however, it is curious that both Rameau[14] and Jean-Jacques Rousseau[15] cite 1700 as the date of the *Traité*. It is clear that Rameau assumes this to be the date of the first edition, because he correctly places the date of the second version as "seven or eight years" before his own *Dissertation* (Paris, 1732).[16] Rousseau duplicates Rameau's inaccurate date, and further adds to the misunderstanding by confusing the two versions. Thinking Delair's discussion of the *rule of the octave* in the *Nouveau traité* to have been published in 1700, he erroneously cites Delair as the first writer to publish the rule. J.J.O. de Meude-Monpas[17] perpetuates Rameau's mistake, as do Choron and Fayolle, who give two separate entries in their *Dictionnaire historique des musiciens* (Paris, 1810),[18] listing both "D. Delair (*Traité*, 1690)," and "Delaire (*Règle de l'Octave*, 1700)."

Harmonist at the Harpsichord (New Haven: Music Theory Translation Series, 1963), pp. 73-75. Kevin Mason has discovered the earliest complete form of the *Rule* in a French manuscript of lute and theorbo pieces compiled by Jean Etienne Vaudry de Saizenay, 1699 (Ms. 279152, Besançon, Bibliothèque Municipale). See Kevin Mason, "François Campion's *Secret of Accompaniment for the Theorbo, Guitar, and Lute*," *Lute Society of America Journal* (1981), vol. 14, p. 73.

[13] " . . . *la Règle de l'Octave . . . Règle presque généralement reçûe, n'a t'elle pris racine en France qu'après l'Edition de ce Traité?*" Rameau, *Dissertation*, p. 7.

[14] Rameau, *Dissertation*, p. 5.

[15] Jean Jacques Rousseau, *Dictionnaire de musique* (Paris: Duchesne, 1768), s.v. "*Règle de l'Octave*," p. 405.

[16] Rameau, *Dissertation*, p. 7.

[17] J.J.O. de Meude-Monpas, *Dictionnaire de musique* (Paris: Chez Knapen et Fils, 1787; facs. reprint Geneva: Minkoff, 1981), s.v. "*Règle de l'octave*," p. 169.

[18] Alexandre Choron and François Fayolle, *Dictionnaire historique des musiciens* (Paris: Chez Valade et Lenormant, 1810), s.v. "Delair (D.)" and "Delaire."

Delair: Composer, Theorist and Teacher of the French Aristocracy

The status of Delair's essay is well documented by his contemporaries, but their accounts reveal little about his actual life. He is listed as a singing teacher on the rue St. Honoré in the 1692 edition of *Le livre commode des addresses de Paris*.[19] This address is confirmed by the title page to the first edition. The dedication of the work to the Marquise Destrades, to whom Delair says he taught voice, suggests that, although he appears to have had no official title, he achieved a measure of success as a singing teacher to members of the nobility. One of Delair's students was possibly Marie-Anne Bloyn; she is listed as the wife of the Marquis Louis d'Estrades (d. 1711), a high-ranking diplomat and soldier, in the *Dictionnaire de biographie française*.[20] The *Nouveau traité d'accompagnement* is dedicated to another of his pupils, la Présidente Saulnier, and cites *l'Hôtel de Créqui* on *rue des Pouliés* as his address.[21] Delair may have been in the employ of one of the resident families of this *hôtel particulier*, providing further evidence that he was being patronized by wealthy and well-born Parisians.

After 1724, there is no record of Delair's activity until 1750, when his name appears on a court document in support of the *harmonistes*, a group of organists, harpsichordists and composers,[22] regarding a parliamentary action which disputes the authority of Jean-Pierre Guignon and the musician's guild called the *ménéstrandise*.[23] Among other protestors was François Couperin, who satirizes the guild in his piece, *"Les Fastes de la grande et anciènne Mxnxstrxndxsx"* (*Onzième*

---

[19]Du Pradel (N. de Blégny, dit Abraham), *Le livre commode des addresses de Paris* (Paris, 1691, 1692); printed in Marcelle Benoit, *Versailles et les musiciens du roi; 1661-1733: étude institutionelle et sociale* (Paris: Editions A. & J. Picard, 1971), Annexe III, p. 413.

[20]*Dictionnaire de biographie française*, direction Roman d'Amat. (Paris VI: Librairie Letouzey et Ané, 1975), vol. 13, p. 138.

[21]With 49 rooms, the *Hôtel de Créqui* was one of the largest of the *hôtels particuliers*, which were almost always home to families of the nobility, magistrate, or financiers. Annik Pardailhé-Galabrun, *La Naissance de l'Intime: 3000 foyers parisiens XVIIe-XVIIIe siècles.* (Paris: Presses Universitaires de France, 1988), p. 241. See also Babelon Gallet, *Demeures parisiennes, l'époque de Louis XVI* (Paris, 1964).

[22]*New Grove Dictionary of Music and Musicians*, Stanley Sadie, ed., s.v. "Delair," by D. Fuller, p. 331.

[23]In 1741, Louis XV appointed Guignon *Roy et maître des Ménétriers, joueurs d'instruments, tant hauts que bas.* This post, vacant since 1695, gave Guignon authority over the *ménéstrandise*, the local musician's union. When Guignon attempted to incorporate keyboardists and composers into the union, they rebelled and were successful in petitioning Parliament to curtail his power. See L. de la Laurencie, "Un musicien piémontais en France au XVIIIe siècle: J.-P. Guignon, dernier *Roy des violons*." *Rivista Musicale Italiana* , vol. 18 (1911), pp. 724, 725.

Ordre), in which he depicts the *ménétriers*, or guild members, as part of a five-act circus show.[24,25] Whether the signator of the court document is the author of the *Traité d'accompagnement* has been questioned. François Fétis gives Delair's date of birth as around 1662; if this is correct, Delair would have been eighty-eight years old at the time of the court proceeding.[26] Apart from his activities as a singing teacher and theorist, he was apparently a composer as well, although the instrumental works mentioned in the royal privilege attached to the *Nouveau traité* have not been discovered.

Synopsis of the *Traité*

As the title indicates, the treatise teaches accompaniment on the theorbo and the harpsichord, the instruments most frequently used for continuo playing, according to Delair. In order to accommodate the impatient beginner, Delair prefaces the body of the work with a ten-page summary, "Principles of Accompaniment for Beginners," which touches on basic principles for realizing figured and unfigured basses. In its succinctness and clarity, the abstract can serve today's novice as an introduction to the art of thoroughbass. Delair explains that these few pages give the player sufficient background to begin accompanying with expediency; the rules encountered further on can be mastered at the student's leisure.

In 1724, Delair inserts a section entitled "General Rules," in which he discusses harmonic *supposition* and the realization of unfigured basses according to the *rule of the octave*.

---

[24]Couperin's program notes detail a procession of minstrels, hurdy-gurdy players, beggars, *jongleurs*, acrobats, and clowns with their bears and monkeys. He makes reference to the earliest minstrels--the French *jongleurs*, or poet-musicians, and the English and German acrobat-musicians, who were "expected to play the drum, cymbals, and hurdy-gurdy; to perform card-tricks and to jump through four hoops. . . ." Willi Apel, *Harvard Dictionary of Music*, Cambridge: The Belknap Press of Harvard University Press (1972), s.v. "Minstrel," p. 531.

[25]Couperin characterizes the guild as inept and unprofessional in the fourth act, which is entitled, "invalids, or crippled people in the service of the grand *Mxnxstrxndxsx*." In the last act, the "disorder and dispersion of the whole troupe caused by the drunkards, monkeys, and bears," Couperin prophesies the break-up of the guild. François Couperin, *Pièces de clavecin*, Second livre (Paris: l'auteur et Foucault, privilège du 14 mai 1713). Ed. Kenneth Gilbert (Paris: Heugel, 1969), pp. 110-117.

[26]François Fétis, *Bibliographie universelle des musiciens et bibliographie générale de la musique*, 2ème éd. (Paris: Firmin Didot Frères, 1866-70), s.v. "Delair," p 454. David Fuller suggests that a son of Delair's may have signed the court action. *New Grove Dictionary of Music and Musicians*, Stanley Sadie, ed., s.v. "Delair," by D. Fuller, p. 331.

The treatise proper begins with a discussion of the rudiments of music. Delair explains the degrees of the scale, accidentals, clefs, keys, and modes, and indicates how to read theorbo and harpsichord tablatures. The rest of the text contains detailed observations concerning figured and unfigured basses, and addresses the topics of transposition and melodic *supposition*. In the addendum from the 1724 edition, Delair updates the *Traité* with remarks on the realization of figured basses using chromatic harmony, the addition of dissonances to unfigured basses, and the harmonization of *points d'orgue*.

Description of Instruments

Harpsichord

It is significant that, of four surviving seventeenth-century French harpsichords examined by Frank Hubbard,[27] three resemble the *clavecin ordinaire* described by Delair, who corroborates that the most common harpsichord was of the "short-octave" variety, with fifty or fifty-one keys and a range of GG to c'''.[28] On seventeenth-century harpsichords, the bass was almost always shortened;[29] the non-chromatic tuning of the lowest strings permitted expansion of the range downward without requiring additional keys. The instrument Delair describes is tuned so that the lowest key, apparent BB, actually sounds GG; apparent C# sounds AA, and the key Eb is tuned to BB. Apparent Eb is sometimes split so that the front half of the key produces the pitch BB and the back half, slightly raised for the convenience of the player, sounds Eb. After C and D, the keys are tuned chromatically. Since the notes GG#, BBb, C# and Eb were seldom employed in music written before the end of the seventeenth century, they were usually omitted from keyboard instruments.[30] Some *clavecins extraordinaires*, Delair reports, had fifty-three keys and a fully chromatic keyboard.

---

[27]These are two-manual instruments, with the range GG/BB to c''', and three registers--2 8' and 1 4'. The earliest is signed *Iacquet Fecit 1652*; another, marked *DESRUISSEAUX*, is thought to date from ca. 1675. The third, which bears the inscription, *Fait par moy Vincent Tibaut a Tolose 1679*, has two split keys in the lowest octave to accommodate AA, C-sharp, BB and E-flat. The fourth harpsichord, G-c''' chromatic, is unsigned and undated, but can be ascribed to the same period because of its range and other similar features. See Frank Hubbard, *Three Centuries of Harpsichord Making* (Cambridge, Mass., 1965), pp. 100-101. Cited by Harris-Warrick, p. 20.

[28]Delair, p. 9 (Mattax, p. 72).

[29]Hubbard, p. 5.

[30]See Raymond Russell, *The Harpsichord and Clavichord* (New York: W. W. Norton, 1973), p. 17.

Another unusual harpsichord had split keys for each accidental. Delair informs us that the difficulty in negotiating the accidentals on these harpsichords made them virtually unplayable.[31] This instrument offers an advantage over the *clavecin ordinaire*. Because there are separate keys for the enharmonic tones, all keys are usable in a meantone temperament, the usual tuning of keyboards in the seventeenth century,[32] as documented by Marin Mersenne,[33] Jean Denis,[34] and Etienne Loulié.[35] The use of split-key accidentals was prevalent in Spain, Italy and Germany as early as the fifteenth century, but it seems, as Delair suggests, that *feintes coupées* were never very popular in France.[36] In his *Harmonie Universelle*, Mersenne describes theoretical instruments with nineteen, twenty-seven and thirty-two notes to the octave.[37] Apparently, Jehan Titelouze owned a spinet which had nineteen notes per octave. Mersenne gives an account of the configuration of the keyboard of this instrument: "One can divide the tone in three equal parts, as Titelouze had done on a particular spinet which he had me hear."[38] (See diagram below of Mersenne's *Clavier Harmonique,* with nineteen keys to the octave.)

In a letter to Mersenne dated March 2, 1622, Titelouze verifies the existence of this harpsichord, which he explains he had built to play chromatic and enharmonic music:

> I could easily send you several four-part pieces in each mode
> . . . . I composed a piece out of curiosity which I play on a
> certain harpsichord made expressly [for this purpose]. . . .[39]

---

[31]Delair, *Traité*, p. 12 (Mattax, p. 75).

[32]In this temperament, the only available chromatic notes are C#, Eb, F#, G#, and Bb. In the twelve-note scale, since enharmonics are not possible--G# cannot serve as Ab, nor D# as Eb--it is evident that the range of harmonic modulation is restricted.

[33]Marin Mersenne, *Harmonie Universelle* (Paris, 1636. Facs. ed. Paris: Éditions du centre national pour la recherche scientifique, 1975), vol. III, p. 341.

[34]Jean Denis, *Traité de l'accord de l'espinette*, (Paris, 1650. Facs. ed. with an introduction by Alan Curtis (New York: Da Capo Press, 1969), p. 14.

[35]Etienne Loulié, *Nouveau système de musique* (Paris: Ballard, 1698), p. 27.

[36]The construction of extravangant keyboard instruments for the purpose of playing chromatic and enharmonic music is detailed as early as 1555 by Nicola Vicentino, who discusses an *archicembalo* with thirty-one keys to the octave. Nicola Vicentino, *L'antica musica ridotta alla moderna prattica* (Rome, 1555. Facs. ed. Kassel: Bährenreiter, 1959). Vido Transuntino built a harsichord according to Vicentino's prescription. See Donald H. Boalch, *Makers of the Harpsichord and Clavichord 1440-1840* (Oxford: The Clarendon Press, 1974), s.v. "Transuntino, Vido," p. 181.

[37]Mersenne, *Harmonie Universelle*, vol. III, pp. 352-357.

[38]*"L'on peut aussi diviser le ton en 3 parties égales, comme avoit fait Titelouze dans une Epinette particulière qu'il m'a fait oüir."* Mersenne, *Harmonie universelle*, vol. II, p. 439.

[39]*"Pour vous envoier quelques consonances à 4 parties en chasque mode, cela se pourroit aisément . . . J'en ay fait quelque piece par curiosité que je touche sur une certaine espinete faite exprez. . . ."* Letter of Jean Titelouze, in Rouen, to Mersenne, in Paris, March 2, 1622.

Clavier Harmonique, Parfait de 19, marches sur l'Octave,
commençant par C sol ut

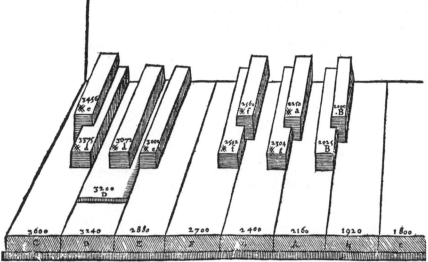

Autre Clavier de dix-neuf marches commençant par F ut fa

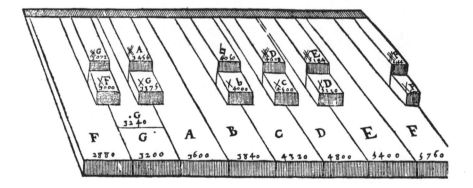

Facsimiles reprinted by permission of Kluwer Academic Publishers from Marin Mersenne,
Harmonie universelle: The Books on Instruments, trans. by Roger Chapman
(The Hague: Martinus Nijhoff, 1957), pp. 435-36

Theorbo

One of the few French theorists to discuss theorbo playing, Delair makes an important contribution to our understanding of theorbo continuo playing in the seventeenth century. That he includes remarks on the theorbo confirms the popularity of hand-plucked instruments in seventeenth-century French ensembles. Despite the greater ease of accompanying on the harpsichord, theorists such as Bénigne de Bacilly and Sébastien de Brossard like the theorbo for its timbre and portability.[40] Bacilly fancies the theorbo even over the harpsichord or the viola da gamba:

> Even the Viol and the Harpsichord do not have the grace or the convenience of the Theorbo, which is suitable for accompanying all sorts of voices . . . By . . . reason of its softness, it accommodates soft and delicate Voices, which the other instruments would obscure.[41]

Brossard insists that the long strings on the theorbo "render the [timbre] so mellow, and cause the sound to last so long, that one should not be surprised if many prefer it to the harpsichord."[42]   Among the hand-plucked instruments, Delair favors the theorbo over guitar and lute:

> Not every instrument is suitable for accompanying since, in accompaniment, the trebles should not dominate the basses. . . . This is the reason one ordinarily does not use the lute or guitar to accompany, since the trebles are too dominant, and the basses not loud enough.[43]

---

[40]Mason, p. 71.

[41]"*La Viole mesme & le Clavessin, n'ont point la grace, ny la commodité qui se rencontre dans le Théorbe, qui est propre pour accompagner toutes sortes de Voix, quand ce ne seroit que par la seule raison de sa douceur, qui s'accomode aux Voix foibles & delicates; au lieu que les autres Instrumens les offusquent.*" Bénigne de Bacilly, *Remarques curieuses sur l'art de bien chanter* (Paris: Ballard et l'auteur, 1668), pp. 17-18.

[42]" *. . . cette longueur en rend le Son si moëlleux, & fait qu'il s'entretient si long-temps, qu'il ne faut pas s'étonner si plusieurs le préfèrent au Clavessin.*" Sebastien de Brossard, *Dictionnaire de musique* (Paris, 1703. Facs. ed. of 1st ed. Amsterdam, 1964, of 2nd. ed. of 1705, Hilversum: Knuf, 1965). English tr. and augmentation by James Grassineau, *A Musical Dictionary* (London, 1740. Facs. ed. New York: Broude, 1966), s.v. "*Theorba*," p. 162.

[43]Delair, *Traité*, p. 5 (Mattax, p. 68).

Delair's description of the instrument conforms to that given by Brossard.[44] Derived from the lute family, the theorbo was single- or double-strung, and had fourteen courses of strings. The top six strings, or *petit jeu*, were tuned in fourths, like the lute, with a third between the third and fourth courses. The neck extended to an extra peg-box for the remaining bass strings, or *grand jeu*, which were twice as long, and tuned diatonically. Delair explains that these strings were not stopped with the left hand, but were plucked by the right thumb and used to play bass notes.[45] Mersenne specifies the tuning of the strings of the theorbo:[46]

Style of Accompaniment

Of particular interest to twentieth-century harpsichordists are Delair's observations about the stylistic aspects of continuo playing. At the outset, Delair recognizes the need to address the "art of accompaniment." Thus, in addition to giving rules for the interpretation of the figures, what Delair calls the "science of accompaniment," he provides insights into the finer points of the style and technique of basso continuo playing. Beyond merely realizing the proper chords above a bass, the accompanist must make artistic decisions concerning the improvisational style. In Delair's opinion, it is this elusive art which, in bringing a piece of music to life, realizes the composer's intentions:

> To be sure, it is difficult to give fixed rules for an art which is based on the [accompanist's ability to interpret] the caprice or the wish of the composer. . . . I hope, nevertheless . . . to clarify the difficulties which are found, giving a complete knowledge of this art, on the theorbo as well as on the harpsichord. . . .[47]

---

[44]Brossard, p. 162. See also Mason, p. 74 and *New Grove Dictionary*, s.v. "Theorbo," by Ian Harwood, James Tyler, and Robert Spencer, p. 740.

[45]Delair, *Traité*, p. 5 (Mattax, p. 68).

[46]Mersenne, *Harmonie universelle*, vol. III, p. 88; Nijhoff ed., p. 116. Facs. reprinted by permission of Kluwer Academic Publishers.

[47]Delair, *Traité*, p. [A] (Mattax, p. 41).

Role of the Accompanist

Defining the role of the accompanist early in the book, Delair states: "It is out of the question to allow the instrument to stand out when accompanying; rather, one should only support the voice one accompanies."[48] As becomes clear by the observations and illustrations given later in the treatise, the subordinate role he assigns to the continuo player does not preclude the embellishment or enrichment of the continuo part. On the contrary, Delair gives the accompanist the freedom to supply ornaments, arpeggiate chords, alter the bass, add dissonances and modify the texture of the realization.

Ornamentation

Delair discusses several ways of decorating the thoroughbass. In his realization of a 5/3 chord, he shows how to diversify the accompaniment, not only by changing the disposition of the chord, but also by adding ornaments. He depicts the essential notes of the chord in arpeggiated whole notes, with eighth and sixteenth notes interspersed at will. These *petites notes* take the form of dissonant passing tones, or *coulés*, which often fill in thirds of chords, and stepwise connecting figures of several notes, or *coulades*. Delair advises the player to hold down all the notes of the chord except the dissonances, which are to be released: "The eighth notes between the whole notes are not absolutely necessary, since they are only for ornament. Thus, one does not hold them, one only passes over them."[49] Jean-Henry d'Anglebert, whose *Principes*[50] predate Delair's *Traité* by one year, also employs ornamental notes. Both authors' examples resemble the *prélude nonmesuré* in style, with arpeggiated chords and a liberal sprinkling of dissonant passing tones.

If the sort of relentless arpeggiation and chaotic embroidery in which Italian continuo players indulged, according to Le Cerf de la Viéville,[51] are not encouraged when performing French music, neither is an overly academic accompaniment. The trend of the day, as corroborated by Delair and d'Anglebert, was toward a richly textured

---

[48]Delair, *Traité*, p. 5 (Mattax, p. 68).

[49]See Delair, *Traité*, pp. [D^v], 30 (Mattax, p. 47, Ex. 4; p. 101, Ex. 112).

[50]Jean-Henry d'Anglebert, *Principes de l'accompagnement*, published in *Pièces de clavecin* (Paris: l'auteur, 1689; ed. Kenneth Gilbert, Paris: Heugel, 1975), pp. 138-145.

[51]*"une espèce de batterie, d'accords, & un harpegement . . . un cahos de sons tricottez & petillans. . . ."* Le Cerf de la Viéville de Freneuse, *Comparaison de la musique italienne et de la musique françoise*, 3 vols. (Bruxelles, 1704-6). Reprinted in Bourdelot's *Histoire de la musique* (1715, later edns. 1721, 1725, 1726, 1743), vol I, pp. 297-298. Cited in Peter Williams, *Figured Bass Accompaniment* (Edinburgh: Edinburgh University Press), vol. I, p. 29.

and florid basso continuo, replete with *coulés* and arpeggios.[52] It is interesting that J.-J. Rousseau, in his *Dictionnaire* of 1752, points to a similarly ornate style of French continuo playing in the eighteenth century: "It is necessary to sustain the Pitches, to arpeggiate them gracefully and continuously from the bottom to the top, always filling in the Harmony, as much as possible. . . . "[53]

Arpeggiation on the Harpsichord

Together with freely arpeggiated chords, Delair depicts metrically broken chords.   In the *Nouveau traité*, to enliven a thinly textured realization when accompanying fast movements, he arpeggiates the notes of the chord in a triplet rhythm.[54]   That Delair added this example in the 1724 edition may be reflective of a change in the style of solo harpsichord music from the elaborate writing of seventeenth-century *préludes nonmesurés* to the lighter texture of rococo *galanteries*.

Arpeggiation on the Theorbo

Bartolotti's *Exemple pour préluder* delineates full-voiced chords arpeggiated both up and down the instrument.[55]   Even if intended primarily to demonstrate how to improvise free preludes, this example shows a type of arpeggiation which was probably also appropriate for continuo playing on the theorbo.   The illustration is consistent with Delair's example of a harpsichord realization which evokes the unmeasured prelude in style.[56]   Campion says to animate the realization with a *batterie*, the technique of strumming transferred to the theorbo from the guitar:

> There is an art to playing chords.   The thumb having played the essential [bass] note, the other fingers should play a *batterie*, alternately re-ascending and multiplying the chord.[57]

---

[52]See d'Anglebert, ed. Kenneth Gilbert, p.vii.

[53]*"il faut soutenir les Sons, les arpéger gracieusement & continuellement de bas en haut, remplir toujours l'Harmonie, autant qu'il se peut. . . .")* Rousseau, *Dictionnaire*, s.v. *"Accompagnement,"* p. 13.

[54]Delair, *Nouveau traité*, p. 67 (Mattax, p. 146, Ex. 223).

[55]Bartolotti, p. 61.

[56]Delair, *Traité*, p. [Dv] (Mattax, p. 30, Ex. 4).

[57]*"Il y a de l'art pour toucher les accords. Le poulce, ayant touché la notte essentielle, les autres doigts doivent faire une batterie en remontant & multipliant alternativement l'accord."* Campion, *l'Addition*, p. 25. Cited by Mason, p. 79.

Alteration of the Bass

Another type of embellishment discussed by Delair is the addition of dissonant passing tones, or *suppositions*, to the bass. The *supposition* is thus named because the dissonant note is said to "suppose" or "substitute" for the displaced consonance. Delair employs *suppositions* to fill in leaps of a third or fourth. These are always preceded and followed by consonances in stepwise motion, in conformance with the rules formulated by René Ouvrard.[58] Recognizing that the accompanist, when ornamenting a bass line, may have difficulty identifying the bass notes on which to play chords, Delair instructs that the chord suitable to the displaced consonance is to be played with the dissonance.[59]

Alteration of the Figures: the Addition of Dissonances to the Realization

In the *Nouveau traité*, Delair goes beyond melodic *supposition*. Inviting the reader to consider harmonic *supposition*,[60,61] he encourages the player to make liberal use of diatonic dissonances such as the seventh and the ninth, even if they are not figured, with the justification that dissonant intervals are merely *suppositions*, substitutions for consonances, and can be applied freely if properly prepared and resolved. He sums up his view in the statement that: "Those skilled in the art [of accompaniment] do not overlook the possibility of playing dissonances that have been prepared, even if they are not figured. . . ."[62] Jacques Boyvin, too, approves of interjecting dissonances if desired:

> . . . Music without dissonance [is] . . . a Soup without salt, a Ragoût without spices, a social gathering without women, & finally, something deprived of all its agreeableness. It is therefore necessary to play Dissonances if one wants to please. . . . These false dissonances, when well managed, make for the beauty and ornament of music: They flatter the ear agreeably, they serve well to express the text in vocal music, and are pleasurable on all sorts of instruments.[63]

---

[58]René Ouvrard, *Secret pour composer en musique* (Paris, 1658), pp. 44ff. Cited in Albert Cohen, "*La Supposition* and the Changing Concept of Dissonance in Baroque Theory," *Journal of the American Musicological Society* 24 (1971), p. 73.

[59]Delair, *Traité*, pp. 60-61 (Mattax, pp. 139-40).

[60]The use of the term *supposition* to mean harmonic dissonance died out with Rameau, who uses *supposition* to mean implied chord-root. See Cohen, p. 77.

[61]Delair, *Nouveau traité*, p. [J] (Mattax, p. 55).

[62]Delair, *Nouveau traité*, p. 71 (Mattax, p. 150).

[63]" . . . *une Musique sans dissonance [est] . . . une Soupe sans sel, un Ragoût sans épices, une Compagnie sans femmes, & enfin, une chose privé de tous ses agréments. Il faut donc faire*

In the concluding pages to the second edition, Delair demonstrates how to spice the thoroughbass with dissonance. For instance, a simple harmonization such as a 6/3 followed by a 5/3 chord may be altered in the following manner: a 6/5 chord is played instead of 6/3 above the first bass note, in order to prepare a 9/4 chord which is then played above the second note, resolving to 8/3 on the last part of the note.[64] Conversely, for the progression of a 5/3 followed by a 6/3 chord over a diatonically ascending bass, the 5/3 chord is replaced by the dissonance, 9/7.[65]

Recitative

Side by side with the ornate style of accompaniment--in which chords are arpeggiated and decorated with passing tones, diminutions improvised in the bass, and dissonances added at the whim of the accompanist--there exists a simpler style, used for fast movements and in recitatives. Delair cautions: "Very few chords are played in fast pieces and in slow recitatives, where chords are separated by some silence in order to feature the voice."[66]

Texture on the Harpsichord

In addition to employing ornaments, harpsichordists may improve their continuo realizations by manipulating the texture. Delair recommends a full-voiced accompaniment for slow movements, and a thinner texture for fast movements:

> There are several ways of accompanying on the harpsichord. Some people play only the bass with the left hand, doing the accompaniments with the right hand. Others play the chords with the left hand as well as the right. To decide between these two ways, I would say that both of them are good, provided that one uses the first manner of accompanying only for basses which are in a fast tempo, and the second manner for those in a slow tempo.[67]

---

des Dissonances si on veut plaire . . . ces Faux-Accords bien menagez font la beauté & l'ornement de la Musique: Ils flattent agréablement l'oreille, ils servent beaucoup à l'expression du Texte dans la Musique vocale, et font plaisir sur toutes sortes d'Instruments." Jacques Boyvin, "Traité abrégé d'accompagnement pour l'orgue et pour le clavessin," *Second livre d'orgue* (Paris: Ballard, 1700). Reprinted in *Archives des maîtres de l'orgue*, ed. by Guilmant and Pirro (Paris: Esching, 1904), vol. 8, p. 74. New York: Johnson Reprint, 1972.

[64]See Delair, *Nouveau traité*, p. 70 (Mattax, p. 149, Ex. 235).

[65]See Delair, *Nouveau traité*, p. 67 (Mattax, p. 145, Ex. 222).

[66]Delair, *Traité*, p. 47 (Mattax, p. 121) For a discussion of French recitative accompaniment, see *New Grove Dictionary*, s.v. "Continuo," by Peter Williams, pp. 694-695.

[67]Delair, *Traité*, p. 57 (Mattax, p. 135).

The filled-in realization is described by d'Anglebert as well, although he warns that a texture of more than four parts is suitable when accompanying slow movements on the harpsichord, but not on the organ: "One can fill in with the two hands on the harpsichord when the tempo is slow, but not on the organ where there must be only four parts."[68] Among the seventeenth-century theorists, Nivers is the only one who requires two voices in each hand: "For perfect harmony, there must be four parts, two in the left hand and two in the right. . . ."[69]

Noteworthy is the fact that most of Delair's examples adhere to four or five parts, with the right hand taking all the notes of the realization. When Delair explicitly notates ornaments and arpeggios to portray the style appropriate for accompanying, he indulges in six and even seven-part chords, with the left hand doubling the bass and the notes of the right hand.[70]

Doubling Voices

For the full-voiced style, Delair permits the doubling of all consonances and all notes of the chords of the second and the tritone (6/4/2 or 6/4#/2 chords), but not of the diminished fifth, seventh or ninth.[71,72] Boyvin, writing in 1700, allows the doubling only of the notes of sixth and second chords.[73] While d'Anglebert does not discuss doublings in his text, his examples show doublings of the chords of the sixth, second and tritone.[74] In one illustration, F. Couperin actually doubles the augmented fifth.[75]

Regarding doublings of sixth and seventh chords in four-part realizations, Delair sets down guidelines which have become standard today. The sixth is ordinarily accompanied by the octave and the third above the bass. However, if a sixth is played on a sharped note, it is preferable to double the sixth.[76] In a sequence of seventh chords over a bass which ascends by a fourth and descends by a fifth, Delair shows the

---

[68] "On peut remplir des deux mains sur le clavecin quand la mesure est lente, mais non pas sur l'orgue où il ne faut que les quatres parties." d'Anglebert, p. 141.

[69] "Pour la parfaite harmonie, il faut qu'il y ait quatre Parties, deux de la main gauche & deux de la main droite..." Nivers, p. 150.

[70] Delair, Traité, p. 30 (Mattax, p. 101, Ex. 112, 113).

[71] Delair, Traité, pp. [Ev-F] (Mattax, p. 49).

[72] George Buelow conjectures that doubling a dissonance such as the tritone was quite bold in seventeenth-century France. George J. Buelow, Thorough-Bass Accompaniment According to Johann David Heinichen (Berkeley and Los Angeles: University of California Press, 1966), p. 70.

[73] Boyvin, p. 75.

[74] d'Anglebert, p. 144.

[75] François Couperin, Règles pour l'accompagnement (Paris: MS, c. 1698). Ed. Oeuvres complètes (Paris: Editions de l'Oiseau Lyre, 1933) vol. 1, p. 14.

[76] See Delair, Traité, p. [E] (Mattax, p. 48, Ex. 9).

seventh, third and doubled octave in one chord, with the fifth omitted, alternating with the seventh, fifth, and third in the other.[77]

Omitting Voices

Delair condones a thinning out of texture for reasons of technical difficulty. He offers more latitude to those using hand-plucked instruments, since, while he urges the theorbo player to use the harpsichord realizations in the treatise as the basis for accompaniment on the theorbo, he recognizes the difficulty of duplicating on the theorbo all the notes a harpsichordist would play:

> It is possible to omit [certain notes in the realization], principally on instruments such as the theorbo--where the hand labors in many places, and one does not find all the desired accompaniments with ease.[78]

When realizing any chord except the 6/4/2 chord, Delair gives the option of playing only the third above the bass. In the same way, he approves of playing only the fourth when it takes the place of the third. In chords whose notes are a third apart, the third may be omitted, such as in 6/4, 7/5, and 8/6 chords.

Texture on the Theorbo

Delair does not include any specific examples of theorbo continuo realizations. In granting the theorbo player license to disregard notes of chords when they are difficult to execute, he implies that continuo realization on the theorbo is somewhat thinner than that on the harpsichord. Campion also countenances leaving out voices if playing them would impede the flow of the continuo line: "We often suppress a part in favor of the well-positioned hand, in order to avoid the frequent displacement of the hand which breaks the connection of the harmony."[79] The three- and four-voiced examples given by Fleury and Henry Grenerin[80] seem to support this. However, full-voiced harmonizations are

---

[77]Delair, *Nouveau traité*, p. 28 (Mattax, p. 98, Ex. 106c).

[78]Delair, *Traité*, p. 31 (Mattax, p. 101).

[79]*"nous supprimons souvent une partie en faveur de la main posée, pour éviter le fréquent déplacement de main qui coupe la liaison de l'harmonie."* François Campion, *Addition au traité d'accompagnement et de composition par la règle de l'octave* (Paris, 1730), p. 9. Cited by Mason, pp. 78-79.

[80]Henry Grenerin, *Livre de Théorbe contenant plusiuers pièces sur différens tons, avec une nouvelle méthode très facile pour apprendre à jouer sur la partie les basses Continues et toutes sortes d'Airs à Livre Ouvert* (Paris: Chez l'Autheur et Bonneuil, ca. 1682. Facs. ed. Geneva: Minkoff, 1984).

found in Bartolotti's *Table pour apprendre à toucher le théorbe*, in which realizations for cadences and recitatives contain five- and even six-part chords.[81]

It is probable that theorbo players doubled notes on other strings to reinforce the sound. Delair shows how to obtain the same pitch on different strings of the *petit jeu*; he also demonstrates the doubling of a note at the octave below on the bass strings of the *grand jeu*.[82]

Selecting the Register

In affirming the importance of the bass over the treble, Delair suggests that basso continuo realizations stayed fairly low on the keyboard. He emphasizes that "it is necessary that the basses dominate."[83] Harpsichordists were fond of exploiting the low resonance of the novel "short-octave" harpsichord;[84] the extended range this instrument offered over previous instruments undoubtedly inspired soloist and continuo player alike. D'Anglebert's illustrations verify the use of a low tessitura,[85] as does Nivers' advice to the accompanist to "assist weak voices by not playing in a high register."[86]

Spacing the Hands

Further reinforcing the assumption that seventeenth-century players preferred to keep their realizations low in range is Delair's admonition to the harpsichordist to keep the right hand as close as possible to the left in order to minimize the gap between the two hands. Should the space between the hands become too great, Delair suggests doubling in the left hand the notes of the chord played by the right.[87] For negotiating a bass which climbs very high, Delair presents a stylish solution: The harpsichordist is to bring the right hand up ahead of the bass, pivoting on a sixth chord, and then reduce the number of parts taken by the right hand as the left hand ascends. The lowest note of the right-hand chord may then be moved up an octave higher. In the subsequent resolution to a

---

[81]Bartolotti, pp. 59-60.
[82]Delair, *Traité*, pp. 5-7 (Mattax, p. 70, Ex. 43).
[83]Delair, *Traité*, p. 5 (Mattax, p. 68).
[84]*New Grove Dictionary*, s.v. "Continuo," by Peter Williams, p. 693.
[85]d'Anglebert, p. 142.
[86]*"Il . . . faut . . . soulager les Voix foibles, en ne faisant pas les Parties si hautes . . ."* Guillaume-Gabriel Nivers, *Motets à voix seule . . . avec l'art d'accompagner sur la basse continue pour l'orgue et le clavecin.* (Paris: l'auteur, 1689), p. 169.
[87]Delair, *Traité*, p. 59 (Mattax, pp. 136-37).

5/3 chord, the octave above the bass is omitted. To give the illusion of a fuller texture, Delair proposes playing a *pincé* on the third of the chord.[88]

Solving Problems of Chord Inversion on the Theorbo

The strings of the *petit jeu* were longer on the theorbo than their counterparts on the lute. Since the top two courses of strings could not withstand the tension of being tuned up to the pitch of their equivalent strings on the lute, they were tuned down an octave, making the third course the highest in pitch. For this reason, chords formed above the third or fourth courses would not sound as written, but would be inverted. It may be that seventeenth-century theorbo players were not overly troubled by mistakes in voice leading or chord inversion resulting from the peculiar tuning of the top strings.[89] Bartolotti, for example, writes out a progression of seventh chords in which the first and third chords are inverted:[90]

Manicre de faire les Septiémes

Transcription:

---

[88]Delair, *Nouveau traité*, p. [L] (Mattax, p. 59).
[89]For a discussion of this issue, see Mason, p. 81 and Nigel North, *Continuo Playing on the Lute, Archlute and Theorbo* (Bloomington: Indiana University Press, 1987), p. 163.
[90]Bartolotti, p. 54.

To correct inversions, Delair simply changes the plucking order of the right hand. He emphasizes that the bass of a chord must always be played first, after which the rest of the notes of the chord may follow in whatever order is convenient:

> One can dispense with following a particular order in playing the notes. Provided that one plays them all, it does not matter what note is played first or last after the bass, which should always precede the [other notes of] the chord. This order is regulated by the convenience of the hand.[91]

Another solution is to transpose down an octave those bass notes that may be too high.

> The theorbo does not have a range that is high enough to supply the compass needed for the treble clefs. One makes up for this defect by taking the treble notes an octave lower.[92]

In Delair's example, all notes above middle C are played down an octave. In addition, players probably doubled notes on the low strings of the *grand jeu* as a remedy for faulty inversions. Delair underscores the fact that the low notes "serve only to fill out [the sonority],"[93] implying that notes were freely doubled on these strings.

Holding Common Chord Tones

Recognizing the importance of holding down the notes common to consecutive chords in order to enhance elegance and sonority in continuo playing, Delair exhorts the accompanist not to repeat notes unnecessarily:

> . . . One may be satisfied with playing, on [bass] notes in the second part of the beat, only the notes that have not been sounded in the preceding chord, holding over those notes from the preceding chord which are appropriate to the following one. For example, when the bass ascends a third, and a sixth is played on the second note, one can dispense with playing any chord on the second note, since all the chord tones above the first bass note are also suitable to the second. It is useless to repeat them, especially when the tempo is fast.[94]

---

[91]Delair, *Traité*, p. [Cv] (Mattax, p. 45).
[92]Delair, *Traité*, p. 6 (Mattax, p. 69).
[93]Delair, *Traité*, p. 6 (Mattax, p. 69).
[94]Delair, *Traité*, p. 50 (Mattax, p. 126).

Avoiding Parallel Fifths and Octaves

Delair gives other practical tips, including procedures for dealing with parallel fifths and octaves. In keeping with standard contrapuntal practice, he recommends contrary motion between the parts, except when the bass leaps by a fourth, in which case similar motion is permitted.[95] Interestingly, he allows two different species of fifth to follow one another in parallel motion. More surprising, however, is his direction that parallel perfect fifths in the right hand may be tolerated if they move in contrary motion with the bass.[96]

To avoid parallels when the bass ascends or descends considerably, Delair shows by his examples how to keep the uppermost voice in about the same range, with chord tones omitted in the right hand as the bass climbs, and added as the bass falls in order to fill in the space between the hands.[97]

Determining When to Play Chords

In general, harmonic rhythm conforms to metrical rhythm, such that chords are confined to the first note of each downbeat (*frapé*) and each upbeat (*levé*). Delair's precepts must be placed in the context of seventeenth-century practice. Brossard describes the convention: "The first [beat] is made by beating or lowering the hand & the second by raising [the hand]."[98] In general, a three-beat measure is conducted by lowering the hand on the first two beats, and raising the hand on the third. Following Delair's advice, in a simple triple meter, chords are played only on the first and third beats of the measure. In compound meters such as 9/8 or 12/8, Delair assigns chords to the first note of every beat. In 6/8, he proposes playing chords on the first and last notes of each downbeat and each upbeat, i.e., on the first, third, fourth, and sixth eighth notes in the bar.[99] The above rules apply only to basses in stepwise motion. Chords are to be supplied on all bass notes which proceed by disjunct degree. On the theorbo, if this is not possible in a fast tempo, it is enough to play chords only on the downbeats and upbeats.

---

[95]Delair, *Nouveau traité*, p. [J] (Mattax, p. 56, Ex. 25).
[96]Delair, *Traité*, p. 44 (Mattax, pp. 117-18).
[97]Delair, *Traité*, pp. 59-60 (Mattax, pp. 137-38).
[98]*"Le premier [temps] se fait en battant ou baissant la main & le second en levant."* Brossard, *Dictionnaire*, s.v. *"Supposition,"* p. 126.
[99]Delair, *Traité*, p. 50 (Mattax, p. 126).

Figured Bass

As Delair notes, one of the first skills an accompanist must acquire when learning continuo realization is the facility to play, at sight, the chords appropriate to a given bass line which, in the seventeenth century, may have been supplied with figures to indicate the notes of the chord, or may have been left entirely unfigured. Since even figured-bass notation was abbreviated to the point that only the figure representing the characteristic interval of the chord was supplied, the player had to learn how to complete the chord. Rameau echoes Delair's frustration concerning the lack of precision in figured-bass notation in his *Dissertation*.[100] A reviewer for the *Journal de Trévoux* eloquently sets forth Rameau's view:

> . . . regarding the 6, Composers will permit us to say that they abuse it completely, that it is their saddle for all horses, & the true occult quality of the Art of music, & by consequence a real stumbling-block for accompanists of good faith. [The 6] is squandered, thrown about, & sometimes you see four or five in a row, which seem to indicate the same chord, & of which there are not two that are not different, one consonant, the other dissonant, all accompanied and matched with different intervals. This one is a 6/4, this one a 6/5, the other a small sixth [6/4/3], and another is a chord of the second [6/4/2].[101]

Delair seems to be the first theorist to devise a table of figured-bass signatures to assist the student in learning the different ways of realizing notated figures.[102] For each of twenty-three chords, he gives the essential figures, those that would be notated on the continuo bass, and, above these figures, numbers designating which additional intervals complete the realization.[103]

---

[100]Rameau, *Dissertation*, p. 3.

[101]". . . *pour le 6, les Compositeurs nous permettront de dire qu'ils en abusent tout-à-fait, que c'est leur selle à tous chevaux, & la vraye qualité occulte de l'Art de la musique, & par conséquent une vraye pierre d'achopement pour les accompagnateurs de bonne foi. On le prodigue, on le jette, & vous en voyés quelquefois des quatre ou cinq de suite, qui semblent tous indiquer le même accord, & dont il n'y en a pas deux qui ne soient différens, l'un consonant, l'autre dissonant, tous accompagnés & assortis de différens intervalles. Celui-ci est sixte quarte, celui là sixte quinte, l'autre petite sixte, & un autre est un accord de seconde."* [*Journal de Trévoux*], 1732, *Mémoires pour l'histoire des sciences et des beaux arts*, January, 1732, vol. 122, p. 450.

[102]Burchill, p. 16.

[103]Delair, *Traité*, p. 29 (Mattax, p. 99, Ex. 110).

Delair divides his realizations of figured basses into two categories: *accompagnements ordinaires*, encompassing for the most part diatonic chords, and *accompagnements extraordinaires*, consisting primarily of chromatic chords.[104] One of the first French theorists to include augmented and diminished chords in his realizations, Delair explains that these false dissonances were generally associated with Italian operatic repertoire.   Along with the Italians, seventeenth-century Spanish composers delighted in chromaticism, as evidenced by the numerous *tientos de falsas*, organ pieces which deliberately exploit chromatic harmony. By contrast, augmented and diminished harmonies were rarely used by French writers such as Jean-Baptiste Lully, whose music was predominantly diatonic. Only with the growing influence of the Italian style on French composition in the eighteenth century did French musicians begin taking advantage of chromatic harmonies in their dramatic pieces.

One of the earliest proponents of such chords as the 4#/3b and 7#/6b,[105] Delair lists six chromatic intervals: the augmented second, augmented fourth, diminished fifth, augmented fifth, diminished seventh, and major seventh.[106] He leaves out only the minor second, diminished third and augmented sixth. In his revised edition, Delair adds the diminished third to his discussion of chromatic harmonies,[107] admitting that most French composers still dislike using it, and protesting that organists have a tendency to omit it when realizing a figured bass. The German theorist, Johann David Heinichen, who gives perhaps the most complete discussion of *falsae* in the eighteenth century, continues to reject the diminished third, charactering it as an "unbearable interval" used by some composers to "express the meaning of harsh words."[108] Nivers mentions twelve augmented and diminished intervals,[109] but does not use any of them in his examples of chordal realizations. F. Couperin is the only other French theorist writing in the seventeenth century to demonstrate the realization of a large number of chromatic chords, including chords of the minor and augmented second, augmented fourth, diminished and augmented fifth, augmented sixth and diminished seventh.[110] Among early eighteenth-century French writers, Boyvin cites only the augmented fourth and diminished fifth,[111] and

---

[104]Delair lists the following *accompagnements extraordinaries*: [2#], [7/4], [4#/3b], [6/5], [8/5b], [7/5b], [7b/5b], [7/5#], [9/5#], [6/4/3], [8/6/4], [7#/4/2], [7#/6b], and [9/7]. See Delair, *Traité*, p. [Fv], (Mattax, p. 51, Ex. 12).

[105]Anderson, pp. 36-37, 44-45.

[106]Delair, *Traité*, p. 16 (Mattax, p. 80).

[107]Delair, *Traité*, pp. 64-65 (Mattax, pp. 142-43).

[108]Buelow, p. 55.

[109]Nivers, p. 150.

[110]F. Couperin, *Règles pour l'accompagnement*, pp. 14-17.

[111]Boyvin, p. 75.

Saint Lambert limits chromatic chords to the augmented fourth, diminished fifth, augmented fifth, and major seventh.[112] If the French generally disparaged dissonances, one would expect Italian essayists to endorse them. Francesco Gasparini is unexpectedly conservative, however. His treatise, which postdates Delair's by some twenty years, ignores the minor second, diminished third, augmented fifth, and augmented sixth.[113] It is a testament to Delair's farsightedness that he includes so complete a discussion of chromatic chords at such an early date.

Delair's realizations of diatonic chords do not differ substantially from those of his contemporaries, although several of his more progressive accompaniments are worth noting. In realizing the chord of a second, he states that 6/4/2, especially in accompanying opera choruses, is more harmonious than 5/4/2, a realization he considers old-fashioned.[114,115] Unique in his treatment of 6/4/3 and 6/4 chords, Delair resolves 6/4/3 by 7/5/3, contradicting Rameau's rule that 6/4/3 must be followed by 5/3.[116,117] His treatment of the 6/4 chord is novel as well. Ordinarily, a sixth preceded by a seventh over the same bass note is accompanied by 8 and 3 (8/6/3). Delair gives the possibility of playing 8/6/4.[118] He also presents alternative realizations for the diminished fifth. Instead of the usual accompaniment of a sixth and a third, he offers the option of playing a diminished seventh with the diminished fifth.[119] When the bass leaps, however, he recommends the accompaniment of the octave and the third.[120]

---

[112]Saint Lambert, *Nouveau traité d'accompagnement du clavecin, de l'orgue, et des autre instruments* (Paris: Ballard, 1707. Facs. ed. Geneva: Minkoff, 1974; later edn. Amsterdam: Roger, c. 1710), p. 11.

[113]Francesco Gasparini, *L'armonico pratico al cembalo* (Venice: 1708. Later edns. Venice: 1715, 1729, 1745, 1764, 1802 and Bologna: 1713, 1722). Trans. by Frank Stillings as *The Practical Harmonist at the Harpsichord* (New Haven: Music Theory Translation Series, 1963), pp. 48-61, as cited in Buelow, p. 62.

[114]Delair, *Traité*, p. 25 (Mattax, p. 91).

[115]Saint Lambert, writing as late as 1707, still expresses a preference for 5/4/2 over 6/4/2, p. 12; Burchill, pp. 44-45.

[116]Delair, *Nouveau traité*, p. 29 (Mattax, p. 98, Ex. 106b). Discussed by Anderson, p. 24.

[117]Rameau, *Traité de l'Harmonie réduite à ses principes naturels* (Paris: Ballard, 1722). Trans. Philip Gossett as *Treatise on Harmony* (New York: Dover, 1971), p. 433.

[118]Delair, *Traité*, p. 28 (Mattax, p. 96, Ex. 101). See Anderson, p. 41.

[119]Delair, *Traité*, p. [Fv] (Mattax, p. 51).

[120]Delair, *Traité*, p. 27 (Mattax, p. 95, Ex. 95).

Unfigured Bass

Harmony by Interval

Following the custom established by Italian writers such as Lorenzo Penna and, later, Gasparini,[121] Delair teaches the accompaniment of unfigured basses by having the student memorize the harmonies appropriate to typical bass progressions, a practice Delair calls *harmony by interval.*

Baroque theorists as late as Carl Philipp Emanuel Bach[122] complained of the difficulties of realizing the unfigured bass, yet its continued use by composers necessitated its inclusion in many of the thoroughbass treatises well into the eighteenth century.[123] Delair, who devotes fully sixteen pages to the unfigured, or partially figured bass, is the first French writer to treat the subject in depth. He gives fifty-three rules showing how to assign figures according to the intervallic motion of the bass. Most of his examples deal with two-note bass patterns, both ascending and descending, although he also includes remarks concerning three-, four-, and five-note progressions.

Delair summarizes basic precepts in the chapter, "Principles of Accompaniment for Beginners," which precedes the main body of the treatise.[124] When the bass ascends a semitone to a bass note on which a 5/3 chord is played, the first bass note will usually be harmonized by a 6/3 chord. The passing tone of a diminished fifth may be played to connect the two chords. For a bass which leaps a third, if the first chord is a 5/3, the second should be 6/3. Upward leaps of a fourth require two 5/3 chords; the passing tone of a seventh may be introduced on the end of the first. When the bass skips a fifth, two 5/3 chords are played, with the passing tone of a sixth played on the end of the first note. Three ascending bass notes are usually harmonized by 5/3, 6/3, and 6/3 chords,[125] while four descending notes are realized by 5/3, 6/4#/2, 6#/3,

---

[121]Lorenzo Penna, *Li prima albori musicali per li principianti della musica figurata* (Bologna: 1672, 1679, 1684, and other editions), chaps. 2-5; Gasparini, chaps. 4-5. Discussed by Buelow, p. 200.

[122]Carl Philipp Emanuel Bach, *Versuch über die wahre Art das Clavier zu spielen* (Berlin: 1759). English translation by William Mitchell, *Essay on the True Art of Playing Keyboard Instruments* (New York: Norton, 1949), pp. 410-411.

[123]Eighteenth-century French writers on the unfigured bass include: Saint Lambert (1707), Jean-François Dandrieu (1719), Michel Corrette (1753), Claude DeLaPorte (1753), and Dubugrarre (1754). Cited by Sandra Mangsen in "The Unfigured Bass and the Continuo Player: More Evidence from France," *Early Keyboard Journal*, Southeastern Historical Keyboard Society, vol. 3 (1984-85), p. 6.

[124]Delair, *Traité*, pp. [GV-I], (Mattax, pp. 52-54, Ex. 15-22).

[125]Delair, *Traité*, p. 35 (Mattax, pp. 107-08, Ex. 129, 130).

and 5/3 chords.[126] Similarly, over five descending notes, 5/3, 6/4#/2, 6/3, 6#/3, and 5/3 chords are played.[127] Over a series of long notes in the bass, if they ascend by step, a sequence of fifth followed by sixth chords may be improvised;[128] if they descend, a sequence of sixth followed by fifth chords, or seventh followed by sixth chords is recommended.[129]

Rule of the Octave

Learning to realize unfigured basses was simplified, in the eighteenth century, by the codification of these rules into a single formula known as the *règle de l'octave*. Inherent in the *rule of the octave* is the recognition of relationships of the degrees of the scale to a given key. As Delair clarifies in the second edition of his treatise, accompaniment using this rule involves playing a 5/3 chord on the tonic and dominant--the notes which establish the key--and a form of sixth chord (6/3, 6/5, or 6/4/3) on all the other degrees. In particular, a 6/4/3 is played on notes which descend to the principal or dominant, and a 6/5 is played on notes which ascend to either of these degrees, although in minor modes Delair prefers 7b/5 to 6/5. Like Campion, Delair's harmonizations of the scale use both diatonic and chromatic chords.[130]

Recognizing the limitations of the rule, Delair makes it clear that he views the formula primarily as a teaching aid. He deprecates those who rely solely on this rule to determine the harmony:

> The *rule of the octave* does not determine the different accompaniments appropriate to [figured] intervals. . . . Thus, it is unreasonable that many people base all accompaniment on the *rule of the octave*, a rule comprising only the smallest part thereof.[131]

In the *Nouveau traité*, Delair appends a variety of additional realizations appropriate to typical bass progressions. In these, he shows how to go beyond the diatonic harmonies required by the *règle de l'octave* to incorporate augmented and diminished chords. Although Delair's prose is sometimes dense and the rules lengthy, his method of harmonizing basses according to the intervallic motion of the bass could be used successfully in teaching today's continuo player how to realize unfigured basses.

---

[126]Delair, *Traité*, pp. 42-43 (Mattax, p. 116, Ex. 162).
[127]Delair, *Traité*, p. 43 (Mattax, p. 116, Ex. 164).
[128]Delair, *Nouveau traité*, p. 67 (Mattax, p. 145, Ex. 222).
[129]Delair, *Traité*, p. 45 (Mattax, p. 120).
[130]Delair, *Nouveau traité*, p. 62 (Mattax, p. 141, Ex. 214).
[131]Delair, *Nouveau traité*, p. [M] (Mattax, p. 61).

Contributions to Music Theory

Delair provides valuable insights into French baroque theory. The chapters devoted to the rudiments of music should not be ignored since, in some sections, he presents, for the first time, certain usages or concepts which are now commonly accepted. For example, he is one of the earliest theorists to prescribe using a natural to cancel a flat.[132] Until Delair, composers used a sharp to cancel a flat. More significantly, he is one of the first writers to mention the double sharp. Apparently, it was such a novelty in France that he must have thought some of his contemporaries might credit him with its invention:

> I know that these double sharped notes will look like a new invention . . . but I would argue that one should not be more surprised to see these notes double sharped than to encounter sharps on *Mi's*, *Si's*, and *La's*, which, being naturally sharped, are nevertheless sharped again. . . . I admit that this is rare, but it is sometimes encountered. I have a printed Italian piece in which there is a *Re* sharp with the major third marked above it, which should be *Fa*, double sharped.[133]

Progressive as well in recognizing the concept of enharmonic equivalence, Delair designs a "Circle of Natural and Transposed Notes" to show how "each degree of the scale can be varied in three or four ways, since it is either natural, flatted, sharped, or sometimes double sharped."[134]

Several of Delair's innovations are conceived as practical devices. For example, to facilitate the process of learning to connect figured-bass signatures with a particular hand position at the harpsichord, he reduces the number of chords the accompanist must learn, by grouping together those that share the same right-hand accompaniment. In this manner, twelve chords relate to the root-position triad (5/3), five to the ninth (9/5/3), four to the diminished fifth (6/5/3), and one to the 5/4-3.[135] For example, a triad above D in the right hand generates a 5/3 chord on D, 6/4/2 on C, 7/5/3 on B-flat, 8/6/4 on A, 8/6/3 on F, and 7/4b/2 on E-flat.

---

[132]Delair, *Traité*, p. 4 (Mattax, p. 68). Burchill credits Delair with being the first to use a natural to cancel a flat, p. 40.

[133]Delair, *Traité*, pp. 11-12 (Mattax, p. 74). Discussed by Anderson, p. 95.

[134]Delair, *Traité*, p. 11 (Mattax, p. 73, Ex. 44).

[135]Delair, *Traité*, p. 30 (Mattax, p. 100, Ex. 111).

The usefulness of this approach did not go unnoticed by later writers, and could be resurrected as a short-cut to learning chords today. Saint Lambert uses Delair's method to associate complicated figures with 5/3 triads above other bass notes, but is less thorough.[136] Rameau, in his *Dissertation*, demonstrates how a seventh chord composed of G, B, D, and F in the right hand yields seven different chords above the bass notes G, B, D, F, C, E, and E-flat. These chords would be figured 7, 6/5, 6/4/3, 4#/2, 7#, 9, and 5#, respectively. Rameau argues that this "labyrinth" of signatures is unnecessary. Since the figures represent inversions of the same seventh chord, one number would suffice.[137] It is possible that the idea of linking chords with the same right-hand realization--which seems to have originated with Delair strictly as a practical device--served as a point of departure for Rameau's theory of chord inversion.[138]

While continuo players struggled to keep pace with the increasing complexity of figures, theorists wrestled with the problem of classifying the new keys being used as their harmonic palette expanded. Delair's theory of modal transposition[139] contributes to our understanding of this categorization, and sheds light on the evolution from mode to key which took place in the late seventeenth century.

In conclusion, with his ideas on chord classification, enharmonic equivalence, chromaticism, transposition, key, and mode, Delair offers a wealth of information about French baroque theory. From the practical standpoint, his treatise has much to teach us about the styles and techniques of basso continuo playing in seventeenth- and eighteenth-century France.

---

[136]Saint Lambert, *Nouveau traité d'accompagnement*, pp. 45-47. Discussed by Burchill, pp. 55, 122.

[137]Rameau, *Dissertation*, pp. 12-13.

[138]Burchill, p. 122.

[139]See Glossary, s.v."*Transposition*."

Annotated Glossary:
Definitions and Historical Perspectives

Accompaniment (*Accompagnement*)

For Delair, *accompagnement* signifies not only the art of improvising above a figured (or unfigured) bass, but refers as well to the intervals (*accompagnements*) which must accompany a figured interval in the realization. Since figured-bass notation was generally abbreviated, the player had to learn what notes or intervals to add to those denoted by the figures given in order to complete the chord. Rameau, in his *Treatise on Harmony*, clarifies:

> . . . In accompaniment, a single figure almost always denotes a chord made up of 3, 4, or 5 sounds. You must therefore be fully aware of the intervals which should accompany each figure, so that you may grasp the construction of a chord as soon as you see the figure denoting it.[140]

Accordingly, the term *accompagnement* has been translated either as accompaniment or interval.

Chord (*Accord*)

Delair is one of the first theorists to differentiate between *intervalle* and *accord*, the former meaning consecutive pitches, or melodic interval, and the latter meaning two or more simultaneous pitches.[141]

---

[140]Rameau, *Treatise on Harmony*, p. 387.
[141]Anderson, p. 9.

Where Delair uses the term *accord* to mean two simultaneous pitches, what is known in modern terminology as harmonic interval, *accord* has been translated as interval rather than chord. Delair makes a distinction between *accord* in composition, a harmonic interval above the bass, and *accord* in accompaniment, the chordal realization of that interval. These terms have been translated as interval and chord, respectively.

Delair also uses *accord* to mean concord, conforming to Brossard's definition of the term--"an assemblage of several sounds heard at once, proportioned such that between them they give pleasure to the ear."[142]

Dissonance (*Dissonance*)

> Just (*Juste*): diationic dissonance, such as the second, fourth, seventh, and ninth.
> False (*Fausse*): augmented or diminished interval.

Harmony (*Harmonie*)

> Natural harmony (*Harmonie naturelle*): diatonic harmony.
> Extraordinary harmony (*Harmonie extraordinaire*): chromatic harmony.
> Harmony by interval (*Harmonie par intervalle*): consonances and diatonic dissonances used to harmonize a partially figured or unfigured bass according to the intervallic motion of the bass line.

Meter, Measure (*Mesure*)

> Ordinary meter (*Mesure ordinaire*): simple meter.
> Extraordinary meter (*Mesure extraordinaire*): compound meter.

Musical measure (*mesure*) in the seventeenth century was associated with the beating of time.[143] Jean Rousseau writes:

> Several ways of beating the measure are used to give diversity to pieces of music, as well as to accommodate the quantity of the

---

[142]" . . . l'assemblage de plusieurs sons entendus tous à la fois, et tellement proportionnés entr'eux qu'ils fassent plaisir à l'oreille." Brossard, *Dictionnaire*, s.v. "*Sysygia*." See also Anderson, p. 9.

[143]Anderson, p. 125.

words, which require sometimes a measure of four counts,
sometimes one of two, or three. . . .[144]

As theorists began to codify the organization of musical measure, they
became concerned with the temporal relationships between note values
within a measure. Loulié defines *mesure* as signifying "a number of equal
beats which serve to regulate the duration of sounds. That is to say,
mesure (meter) serves to apply time to notes, more or less in proportion to
their values."[145] Yet, Loulié also continues to define *mesure* as measure,
that is, "the duration of time from one down-beat to the next." By
Delair's time, *la mesure* was the determinant not only of rhythmic
organization, but also had implications for tempo[146] and even *affect.*[147]
Charles Masson describes the affective quality of *mesure*:

> *Mesure* is the soul of music, since it makes a great number of
> persons react with such specificity, and since by means of the
> variety of its movements it can also arouse many different
> passions, being able to calm some and excite others, as has
> always been observed.[148]

Mode (*Mode*):

By Delair's time, the transition from the church modes to the
major/minor system had nearly been completed. Masson, who is among
the first theorists to embrace the major/minor system, writes that the
major and minor modes " . . . encompass all that Antiquity has taught and

---

[144]"*On se sert de plusieurs manières de battre la Mesure pour diversifier les Pièces de
Musique, comme aussi pour s'accommoder à la quantité des paroles, qui demande tantost une
Mesure à quatre temps, tantost à deux, tantost à trois, etc.*" Jean Rousseau, *Méthode claire,
certaine et facile, pour apprendre à chanter la musique.* (Paris, 1678; 5th ed. rev. and aug.,
Amsterdam, ca. 1710), p. 86. Cited by Betty Bang Mather, *Dance Rhythms of the French
Baroque* (Bloomington: Indiana University Press, 1989), p. 53.

[145]Etienne, Loulié, *Elements ou principes de musique mis dans un nouvel ordre* (Paris:
Ballard et l'auteur, 1697). Trans. and ed. by Albert Cohen as *Elements or Principles of Music*
in *Musical Theorists in Translation*, vol. VI (New York: Institute of Mediaeval Music, 1965),
p. 26.

[146]For a discussion of the relationship between meter signs and tempo in the
eighteenth-century France, see George Houle, *Meter in Music 1600-1800* (Bloomington:
Indiana University Press, 1987), pp. 36-38.

[147]See Mather, pp. 55-6.

[148]"*La Mesure est l'âme de la Musique, puisqu'elle fait agir avec tant de justesse un
grand nombre de Personnes, & que par la variété de ses mouvemens elle peut encore émouvoir
tant de différentes passions, pouvant calmer les unes & exciter les autres, ainsi qu'on l'a
toujours remarqué.*" Charles Masson, *Nouveau traité des règles pour la composition de la
musique* (Paris, 1699. Facs. ed. with an intro. by Imogene Horsley New York: Da Capo Press,
1967), p. 6.

even the eight tones sung in church. . . ."[149] Similarly, Michel l'Affilard states clearly that "all the modes or tones in music can be reduced to two-- the major and minor modes."[150] For many French theorists in the seventeenth century, the terms *mode* and *tone* were synonymous. Masson writes that "mode or tone is the manner of beginning, conducting, and concluding an Air on certain pitches appropriate to each mode or tone." He goes on to explain why these terms are interchangeable. "The Ancients used the term mode," he says, "but most Moderns use tone in place of mode because of their relation to the different types of ecclesiastical chants which are called *tones*."[151] With Saint Lambert, a clear differentiation is made between tone, the tonic note, and mode, the intervallic species (major and minor).[152] Delair makes a similar distinction, stating that, "to ascertain the [key] of a composition, one looks at the final. . . . To know if the composition is major or minor, one observes the third of the last note."[153] His avoidance of the terms tone and mode in this passage demonstrates the confusion surrounding their usage. Terminology was codified by Rameau, who writes that the tone, meaning the key of a piece, is determined by its tonic note, and its mode-- whether major or minor.[154] Delair conforms to this usage in the second edition, so that tone means key in the modern sense and, accordingly, has been translated as such. In the first edition, the term tone is not used uniformly and therefore has been translated alternately as mode or key, depending on context.

Modulation (*Modulation*)

Delair uses the term *modulation* to refer to the configuration of tones and semitones within the octave, not, as it is used in the modern sense, to mean a change of key. Brossard confirms the term's meaning in seventeenth- and eighteenth-century France: " . . . to modulate, according

---

[149] " . . . ces deux Modes . . . renferment tout ce que l'Antiquité a enseigné, & mêmes les huit Tons que l'on chante dans l'Eglise. . . ." Masson, p. 9.

[150] "Tous les Tons, ou Modes de la Musique se peuvent réduire à deux; sçavoir au Ton majeur, & au Ton mineur." Michel l'Affilard, *Principes très faciles pour bien apprendre la musique* (Paris: Ballard, 1694; reissued 1697, 1700, 1701, 1702, 1705, 1707, 1711. Facs. of 1705 ed. Geneva: Minkoff, 1971), p. 11.

[151] "Par le mot de Mode ou Ton, on entend la manière de commencer, conduire & conclure un Air sur certaines cordes ou notes propres à chaque Mode ou Ton. Les Anciens se servoient du terme de Mode, mais la plus grande partie des Modernes ont mis en usage celuy de Ton en la place de celuy de Mode, à cause que les différentes manières des Chants de l'Eglise s'appellent Tons." Masson, p. 9.

[152] Saint Lambert, *Nouveau traité de l'accompagnement*, p. 26.

[153] Delair, *Traité*, p. 52 (Mattax, p. 129).

[154] Rameau, *Treatise on Harmony*, trans. Gossett, p. liv.

to modern [composers], is . . . to have a melody proceed by the essential and diatonic notes of the mode."[155]

Movement (*Mouvement*)

The term *mouvement* in French baroque theory refers to the expression as well as the tempo of a piece.[156]   Bacilly says that "*mouvement* is . . . a certain quality which gives spirit to a song . . . and inspires in the hearts [of the listeners] whatever passion the singer might want to bring forth."[157]

Natural chord (*Accord naturel*)

The natural chord is the major or minor triad in the 5/3 position. Rameau and Saint Lambert refer to this chord as the perfect chord (*accord parfait*), but Delair opposes the use of the word perfect: "It is wrong to call this chord perfect since the third often changes, being sometimes major and sometimes minor."[158]

Organ Point (*Point d'orgue*)

The *point d'orgue* is a long note in the bass, over which a series of chords are played.   J.-J. Rousseau clarifies:

> We generally call *points-d'Orgue* those types of pieces, whether measured or not, written out or not, [which call for] harmonic successions [to be] played above a single note of the Bass, which is always prolonged.[159]

Delair describes dominant and tonic pedals harmonized by alternating 5/3 and 7/4/2 chords or a longer sequence of dissonant chords.[160]

---

[155] *"moduler selon les Modernes, c'est . . . faire passer un Chant par les Chords essentielles & naturelles d'un mode."* Brossard, *Dictionnaire*, s.v., "Modulation," p. 53.

[156] Anderson, p. 135.

[157] *"Le Mouvement est . . . une certaine qualité qui donne l'âme au Chant . . . elle inspire dans les coeurs telle passion que le Chantre voudra faire naistre."* Bacilly, p. 200.   See Anderson, p. 135.

[158] Delair, *Traité*, p. 23 (Mattax, p. 89).

[159] *"C'est relativement à cette espèce de Point qu'on appelle généralement points d'Orgue ces sortes de Chants, mesuré ou non mesurés, écrits ou non écrits, & toutes ces successions harmoniques qu'on fait passer sur une seule note de Basse toujours prolongé."* Rousseau, *Dictionnaire*, s.v. *"Point d'orgue,"* p. 380.

[160] Delair, *Nouveau traité*, pp. 69-70 (Mattax, pp. 148-49).

Rule of the Octave (*Règle de l'octave*)

A scale harmonization formula used for accompanying unfigured basses, this rule involves playing a 5/3 chord on the tonic and dominant, and a form of sixth chord (6/3, 6/5, or 6/4/3) on all other scale degrees. Rousseau attributes the invention of the *règle* to Campion, although Campion himself credits his teacher, M. de Maltot with its invention. The *Rule of the Octave* ". . . is a secret which was given to me by the illustrious M. de Maltot, my predecessor at the Royal Academy of Music. He invented it and entrusted me with it."[161] Although in fact Campion was the first to publish the rule in France (*Traité*, 1716), a complete version of it is found in a French manuscript of lute and theorbo pieces dated 1699.[162] Its wide acceptance prompted writers such as Delair and Campion to include it in the second editions of their *Traités*; Rameau goes so far as to claim that it was Delair's publication of the *règle* which made it popular in France.[163] Campion lauded the adoption of the rule for its efficacy in teaching the realization of unfigured basses.[164] By contrast, Delair considered it overly simplistic and cautioned players not to limit themselves to the harmonies required by the formula.

Supposition (*Supposition*)

Supposition, meaning the substitution of a dissonance for a consonance, originated in Italian theory at the beginning of the 17th century. It is first mentioned as a means of dissonance control in Giovanni Maria Artusi's *Delle imperfettioni della moderna musica* (Part I, 1600; Part II, 1603).[165] In the first edition of his *Traité*, Delair uses the term *supposition* in a melodic context to mean a dissonant passing tone added to a bass melody. The dissonant note is said to "suppose" or "substitute" for the displaced consonance. In the *Nouveau traité*, Delair introduces the concept of harmonic *supposition*, in which the harmony may be enriched by playing dissonant chords in the place of consonant ones. Rameau's employment of *supposition* to mean implied chord root represents a different usage of the term.

---

[161]François Campion, *Addition au traité d'accompagnement par la règle de l'octave* (Paris, 1730), p. 4. "*C'est le secret que m'a donné l'illustre M. de Maltot mon prédécesseur en l'Académie Royale de Musique. Il l'a inventé, & m'en a fait dépositaire.*" Cited and tr. by Mason, p. 73.

[162]Cf. fn. 12.

[163]See Commentary, pp. 3-4.

[164]Campion, *Addition*, pp. 3-4.

[165]Cohen, p. 65.

Syncopation (*Syncope*)

Syncope, as used by Delair, has the implication of both suspension and dissonance. For example, in several of Delair's examples, a dissonant chord such as the tritone (6/4#/2) is introduced over the second half of a suspended bass note (*basse syncope*) which subsequently resolves down by step. This is consistent with Gioseffo Zarlino's usage of *syncope* to mean dissonant suspension in a harmonic context. Because the term, *suspension*, did not enter French musical vocabulary until Rameau's time,[166] Delair's original wording has been retained in the translation.

Tone (*Ton*)

According to Loulié, the term tone has several meanings:

1. Tone signifies a certain distance or interval between consecutive pitches, as from *Ut* to *Re*. 2. Tone signifies what musicians call mode. 3. Tone signifies pitch.[167]

Correspondingly, this term has been translated as tone, mode or key, and pitch, respectively, depending on context.

Transposition (*Transposition*)

As the tonal universe expanded, theories of modal transposition evolved to explain and categorize the new keys being used.[168,169] In the first part of his treatise,[170] Delair uses the term *transposition*[171] as we use it today--the rewriting or "performance of a composition in another

---

[166]Anderson, p. 186.

[167]"*Le mot de Ton a plusieurs Significations. 1o. Ton signifie une certain distance ou Intervalle d'un Son à un autre Son, comme d'Ut à Re. 2o. Ton signifie ce que les Musiciens appellent Mode. On a parlé cy-devant du Ton comme Intervalle & comme Mode. 3o. Ton signifie un Degré de Son déterminé.*" Loulié, *Elémens*, p. 77.

[168]See Robert Bates, *From Mode to Key: a Study of 17th-Century French Liturgical Organ Music and Music Theory*, Ph.D. Diss., Stanford University, 1986.

[169]The idea of considering as transposed those modes that have chromatic notes is not new in Delair's time. Just as seventeenth-century theorists attempted to classify keys with increasing numbers of accidentals, so medieval scholars tried to adjust chants with chromatic notes to fit into the eight-mode system. They devised a theory of "affinities," in which chants with chromatic inflections such as E-flat and F-sharp were transposed. In this way, unacceptable sharped or flatted notes could be changed by means of B-flat so that they conformed to the diatonic hexachord. The note on which these transposed modes ended was called the *affinalis* since it was considered a note "in affinity with the standard modal final." Dolores Pesce, *The Affinities and Medieval Transposition* (Bloomington: Indiana University Press, 1987), p. 2.

[170]Delair, *Traité*, p. 10 (Mattax, p. 73).

[171]Delair, *Traité*, p. 10 (Mattax, p. 73, Ex. 44).

key."[172] According to Jean Rousseau, the accompanist should be able to transpose into many modes to accommodate singers.[173]

Later in his treatise, Delair gives another explanation of transposition, stating that it is the position of the third above the final which determines whether or not a mode is transposed. If the third falls on a natural note, the mode is natural; if it falls on an accidental, the mode is transposed. Accidentals on other notes may appear in the key signature without signifying transposition.[174] Delair lists fourteen keys, two on each natural note from C to A, one on B flat (B flat major), and one on B natural (B minor). The number of keys available is restricted by meantone temperament. For example, B major is not usable because the third of the key, D#, would be out of tune in a meantone temperament.

In basing his criterion for transposition on the third, Delair is like Jacques Ozanam and Jean-Pierre Freillon-Poncein,[175] who also base their systems of transposition on the principal degrees of the scale. Ozanam divides the modes into three groups. The first two contain the natural modes. These are divided into those modes which have both their final and their diatonic third on natural notes (except for B flat, which is also included in this category), and those which have their final on a natural note, but their third on an accidental. The third group contains the transposed modes, which include those modes which have both their final and their third on an accidental.[176] For Freillon-Poncein, the final alone determines whether or not a mode is transposed. The mode is natural if its final is found on a natural note. This allows many more natural modes than were permitted in the systems of Delair and Ozanam. Freillon-Poncein divides the transposed modes--those modes with finals on accidentals--into two groups: Those with thirds on sharped notes are called *transposées par b. quarre*, and those with thirds on flatted notes are called *transposées par b. mol*. Freillon-Poncein is the first to introduce all forty-two keys--the major and minor keys and their enharmonic equivalents.[177]

---

[172]Apel, *Harvard Dictionary*, p. 860.

[173]Jean Rousseau, *Traité de la viole* (Paris: C. Ballard, 1687), pp. 116-17.

[174]Delair, *Traité*, pp. 52-53 (Mattax, pp. 129-30).

[175]Jacques Ozanam, *Dictionnaire mathématique* (Paris: E. Michallet, 1691), s.v. "Musique," pp. 640-672; Jean-Pierre Freillon-Poncein, *La véritable manière d'apprendre à jouer en perfection du hautbois, de la flûte, et du flageolet* (Paris: Collombat, 1700. Facs. ed. Geneva: Minkoff, 1974), p. 6.

[176]Ozanam, p. 659-60.

[177]Freillon-Poncein, pp. 51-53.

Treatise of Accompaniment for the Theorbo, and the Harpsichord

Which contains all the rules necessary to accompany on these two instruments. With particular observations concerning the different styles suitable to them. The treatise also teaches to accompany unfigured basses.

Written by D. DELAIR

Sold in Paris, at the author's residence, *Rue St. Honoré*,

near the *Croix du tiroir*, opposite the

Hotel d'Aligré à l'Ecouvette

1690

TRAITÉ D'ACOMPAGNEMENT

POUR LE THEORBE, ET LE CLAVESSIN.

Qui comprend toutes les régles necessaires,

pour aconpagner sur ses deux Jnstruments,

Avec des observations particulieres touchant les

Differentes manieres qui leurs conviennent

Il enseigne aussi à Acompagner les basses qui ne sont pas chifreez.

COMPOSÉ PAR D. DELAIR.

Se vend à Paris Chez l'Auteur Rüe S.ᵗᵉ Honoré proche la Croix du tiroir,
vis à vis l'Botel d'Aligre à l'Ecouvette

1690

Roußet Sculpsit

To Madame the Marquise Destrades

Madame,

The work which I take the liberty to present to you justifiably belongs to you alone, and would never have been put in a publishable state, had you not wished that I teach you accompaniment, having taught you music and singing. In writing it, I intended to assist you in acquiring the knowledge of an art which includes all that is the most difficult in music, and to show you by this small attention that I do not neglect anything, so that I might merit the benevolence and protection with which you have always honored me. Thus, Madame in fulfilling my duty, giving public testimony of my gratitude, I am well-pleased to adorn my work with your illustrious name. Someone else would have taken this occasion to give you eulogy. This noble exterior, this perfect beauty with which you are graced, a noble and refined mind, a sincere and generous heart, and a thousand other fine qualities which are admired in you--these would furnish an ample subject for justifiable praises, but a respectful silence seems to me more appropriate to what I owe you. I will content myself to beseech you to accept that I continue to call myself with deep respect,

Madame,

Your very humble and very obedient servant,

DELAIR

Extract of the Privilege of the King

By patented letters of His Majesty, given at Versailles on June 19, 1690, it is permitted that Mr. Delair engrave, print, sell and stock a book entitled *Treatise of Accompaniment for the Theorbo and the Harpsichord*. It is strictly forbidden for anyone, whatever his title or rank, to engrave, print, sell, stock or counterfeit this book, under any pretext, during the next eight years, or he will face a penalty of three thousand pounds, confiscation of the copies, and all expenses, losses, and interests, as it is declared at greater length, in the letters of Privilege.

Printed the eighth of August, 1690.
Copies were provided.

Preface[178]

[A]

Accompaniment has never been as widespread as it is today. Almost all those who play instruments dabble in accompanying, but very few accompany correctly. Most are contented to follow a certain routine performance, which, not being supported by the science of accompaniment, does not prevent their committing numerous errors--errors which are all the more unavoidable, since they are not perceived. This has come about because no one, up to the present, has treated the subject of accompaniment in depth, either because there are few people who wish to take the trouble to learn all the rules necessary to accompany perfectly, or because most have learned to accompany by rote, and teach it in the same way.

To be sure, it is difficult to give fixed rules for an art which is based on [the accompanist's ability to interpret] the caprice or wish of the composer. In fact, accompaniment should relate to all the parts accompanied; the accompanist is obliged to play, on the spot, appropriate chords which a composer would have notated only with a great deal of time, trouble and travail. I hope, nevertheless, by the rules which I give, to clarify the difficulties which are found, giving a complete knowledge of this art, on the theorbo as well as on the harpsichord, the two instruments most frequently used for accompaniment.

[B]

So that nothing is omitted, I will begin with the rudiments of music, explaining the scale, the notes, and the clefs, as notated and as played on these two instruments. I have separated what is appropriate to each instrument specifically, beginning with the theorbo--showing the strings,

---

[178]Bracketed letters and numbers to the right of the page correspond to pages in the original French *Traité*.

the tablature used to indicate the notes, the clefs, and a summary for finding all the notes, natural as well as sharped or flatted, and played in all possible ways. This knowledge, being the foundation for [playing] chords, will greatly facilitate accompaniment. After this, I proceed to the harpsichord--showing the number of keys it contains, the differences between them, and what they signify with respect to [written] music. I explain the degrees of the scale, the notes, and the clefs for this instrument. Next, I show a double circle, which will give a complete understanding of the keyboard, and of the natural as well as transposed modes. Following this, I discuss the principles of composition, which serve as a foundation for accompaniment in general, on any instrument, and demonstrate the principle of chords, and of what they are composed.

One may find, perhaps, that these principles resemble those that another composer has put in his treatise of composition, yet this composer does not pretend, any more than myself, to be the author. These principles, being fundamental to music, have been established since the invention of music; I have included them because order requires it. [However], one will see by my particular observations, that I have not followed the opinions of others.

Next I discuss [harmonic] intervals (*accords*), which can be clearly understood by means of a sort of dial, which I invented several years ago and have inserted in this treatise; this dial contains all possible intervals, in natural as well as transposed modes. Then I show how these intervals are notated above continuo basses, and with what they are accompanied. These principles will be learned, not only from the discussion which deals with the accompaniment of each particular interval, including exceptions to the rules, but also from the examples at the end of each explanation. Separate letters in the text refer to the musical examples which, marked with the same letters, substantiate the discussion. I frequently put figures on these examples. I also intentionally suppressed them at times, so that one does not rely entirely on the figures, but reflects on the rules. [In this way], one accompanies by thinking and not by rote. It seemed to me all the more useful that most of the intervals relating to the rules I discuss not be figured above the continuo bass. After having presented the rules for ordinary as well as extraordinary accompaniments, I give principles for accompanying unfigured basses, and, so as to proceed in an orderly manner, I demonstrate what one should do on each interval of the bass, ascending and descending.

[B^v]

I know that these rules cannot be completely universal. There will be some situations which do not conform to the rules, as, for example, when one finds the major third with the minor sixth, the tritone with the minor sixth, diminished or augmented octaves, and several other accompaniments which are found in Italian music. Since these accompaniments or chords are based on caprice, not being established according to the rules, I did not believe I should give them as principles.

After acquainting [the reader] with the notes, intervals, chords, and their accompaniments above figured and unfigured basses, I proceed to an explanation of meter--demonstrating, by their different signs, the difference between ordinary and extraordinary meters.[179] After demonstrating the value of notes and rests in relation to these meters, I point out the notes on which one should play a chord, and those one should merely pass over. Then I teach how to ascertain the [key],[180] that is, the degree of the scale and the mode, major or minor, of the piece being accompanied.

Following this, I discuss transpositions, giving the reason for all the sharps and flats after the clef in transposed modes, and, so as to proceed with order, I take all the keys which are in use, one after the other, showing, according to principles, the notes which should be sharped or flatted naturally in each particular key.

[C]

This knowledge is necessary in the accompaniment of Italian music, in which the sharps and flats in transposed modes are not marked. Next, I give several rules concerning the manner of accompanying on the harpsichord--rules for the position of the hands as well as the disposition of the chords, and rules for finding the chords in transposed modes easily. I conclude by giving several rules for *suppositions*. Thus, I think that I have omitted nothing which concerns accompaniment.

In the rest of the treatise, one will see specific comments which regard the theorbo and the harpsichord separately, although the body of the work concerns the harpsichord more than the theorbo because of the greater ease of accompanying with perfection on the harpsichord.

To make expedient use of the treatise, one should not proceed to the next rule without understanding the preceding one. There is nothing useless or out of sequence; thus, in order to accompany perfectly, one should know all that this volume contains.

[C^V]

It might be tedious to [begin] accompanying only after [acquiring] a knowledge of this treatise; therefore, I have put into abbreviated form

---

[179]Simple and compound meters.

[180]Delair speaks of *"la manière de connoitre en quoi est la pièce,"* avoiding the use of the the the term *ton* (meaning key). Our modern terminology was not yet codified; Saint Lambert is the first French theorist to differentiate *ton*--the tonic note--from *mode*--the intervallic species. Discussed by Anderson, pp. 127-130.

the principal rules which one can practice. Meanwhile, one will learn at one's leisure the detailed observations which are found in the work.

All the rules should be observed on any instrument one might wish to use for accompanying, be it lute, guitar, double lute or other instrument, except for several remarks pertaining specifically to the theorbo and harpsichord.

Those who find something that confuses them in the treatise have only to do me the honor of consulting me, and I will resolve their difficulties.

Advice

Before accompanying, one must know the notes and clefs that will be used, both [as notated] on paper, and [as played] on the instrument. Concerning this topic, one should first read the pages of the treatise which teach the principles of music. Those who wish to accompany on the theorbo should read and learn the first seven pages, and those who wish to accompany on the harpsichord should read until the end of the twelfth page, leaving out the three pages that concern only the theorbo. After this, the principles which follow should be learned.

One will observe that the tablature I have employed for the harpsichord serves also for the theorbo, since, on the theorbo, one is obliged to play as much as possible all the notes found in the harpsichord tablature. Nevertheless, one can dispense with following a particular order in playing the notes. Provided that one plays them all, it does not matter what note is played first or last after the bass, which should always precede the [other notes of] the chord. This order is regulated by the convenience of the hand.

Principles of Accompaniment for Beginners

There are eight intervals (*accords*) in accompaniment, namely, the second, the third, the fourth, the fifth, the sixth, the seventh, the octave and the ninth. These are indicated by a figure, which expresses the number of degrees each interval contains. For example, the second is indicated by a two, because it contains two degrees; the third is indicated by a three, because it contains three degrees; the fourth, fifth, sixth, seventh, eighth and ninth are indicated in like manner.

To find an interval above the bass, one must count in ascending, not in descending, order. Thus, to find the third above *Ut*, one counts *Ut, Re, Mi* and not *Ut, Si, La*. It is the same for the other intervals.

A sharp after a figure renders the interval signified by this figure sharped or major. Thus, a sharp after a six indicates a major sixth.

Ex. 1

A flat after a figure renders the interval signified by this figure flatted or minor. Thus, a flat after a six indicates a minor sixth.

Ex. 2

The sharps or do not, in any way, render the fourth, fifth, or octave major or minor, but rather make them augmented or diminished.

A single sharp above or below a note indicates the major third. A single flat above or below a note indicates the minor third.

Ex. 3

The most common chord is the natural chord,[181] which consists of the third, the fifth, and the octave. The natural chord is encountered in six different notations: that is, when nothing is marked above the bass, or when there is a "three," a "five," an "eight," a sharp or a flat--the difference being that a sharp or a flat changes the nature of the third of the chord, rendering it major or minor. One will see in the following example all the ways in which the natural chord can be diversified. The eighth notes between the whole notes are not absolutely necessary, since they are only for ornament. Thus, one does not sustain them, one only passes over them.[182]

[D^V]

Ex. 4

Before proceeding to the following examples, one must learn all the ways of playing the natural chord on each particular note of the scale, until one finds it easily.

The second is ordinarily accompanied by the fourth and sixth (A). Sometimes, the second is also accompanied by the fifth (B).

Ex. 5

The fourth preceded by a third on the same [bass] note is accompanied by the sixth and the octave (A); a fourth followed by a

---

[181]As Delair clarifies in Chapter IV, "The Manner in Which to Mark Chords on the Continuo Basses," the natural chord is the major or minor triad in the 5/3 position. Note Delair's justification for using the term, "natural," rather than "perfect," the word coined by his contemporaries.

[182]The resemblance of Delair's example to the *prélude nonmesuré* in the use of *coulés*, or passing tones, and arpeggiation, attests to the floridity of basso continuo realizations in seventeenth-century France.

third on the same note is accompanied by the fifth and the octave (B); and the fourth alone on a note is accompanied by the second and the sixth (C).

Ex. 6

[E]

The sharped, or augmented, fourth which is called the tritone, is ordinarily accompanied by the second and the sixth (A,B). It is also accompanied by the sixth and the octave, when it occurs on the second half of a note which is not a suspension (C,D).

Ex. 7

The flatted, or diminished, fifth, which is called the false fifth, is accompanied by the third and the sixth when the bass ascends by semitone (A). In all other cases, it is accompanied by the third and the octave (B,C).

Ex. 8

The sixth is accompanied by the third and the octave when it occurs on a note that is not sharped (A,B). However, when it occurs on a sharped note, it is accompanied only by the third and the sixth, doubled (C).

Ex. 9

[E^V]

The seventh is ordinarily accompanied by the third and the fifth.

The ninth is accompanied by the third and the fifth.

One may double in the left hand all the consonances which belong to figured intervals and their accompaniments. One may even double the intervals which accompany the second, including the second itself. One may also double the intervals which accompany the tritone, along with the tritone. However, one does not double the diminished fifth, the seventh, or the ninth.[183]

[F]

One should study the preceding rules on all the notes until all chords are easily found, since accompaniment consists not only in the science of accompaniment, but in the application and use as well.

While practicing these principles, one will learn at one's leisure what is contained in this treatise. By resuming the treatise at the thirteenth page, which teaches the principles of composition, and continuing on, one will see the preceding rules explained at length, with their exceptions. Then, from the twenty-third to the twenty-ninth pages, one will find still more [figured] intervals and other extraordinary accompaniments.

Because I have not put into tablature the examples of these extraordinary accompaniments, having included after their explanations

---

[183]Delair refers to the full-voiced style of accompaniment in which the left hand doubles the notes of the right. That he feels it necessary to include rules for doubling in this summary suggests that harpsichordists liked to take advantage of the sonorous potential of the keyboard by playing full chords in both hands. In Chapter VIII, "General Rules Concerning the Manner of Accompanying on the Harpsichord," Delair explains the contexts in which the filled-in accompaniment is appropriate.

only what is found on the figured basses, I thought I should include them here, so that those who may find something which troubles them, will have recourse to these examples.

Extraordinary intervals and accompaniments include the augmented second, the fourth with the seventh, the tritone with the major or minor third, the fifth with the sixth, the diminished fifth with the octave (or with the diminished or natural seventh), the augmented fifth with the seventh or ninth, the sixth with the third and the fourth (or with the fourth and the octave), the major seventh with the second and the fourth (or with the minor sixth), and the ninth with the seventh.

All these accompaniments are illustrated in the examples following.

See Ex. 12: *Extraordinary Accompaniments*

Below is another progression which shows examples of most of the preceding chords, as well as of others, such as the diminished fifth with the natural seventh:[184]

[G]

Ex. 13

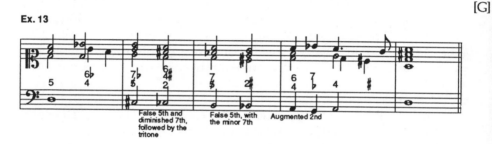

I notated most of the preceding examples in only one manner. Because the notes of the chords are always the same, the chords can be varied only by transposing the parts, putting the highest on the bottom, and the lowest on top, according to the various dispositions of the hand. Thus, provided that the chord tones of each realization are found, it does not matter which is the highest or the lowest. One determines which notes should enter into each chord and then plays them in the manner that falls best under the hand, practicing contrary motion between the bass and other parts as much as possible.

The treatise will demonstrate the different situations in which these extraordinary accompaniments are used.

---

[184]This page is bound incorrectly in the Minkoff edition, with *verso* preceding *recto*.

Ex. 12: *Extraordinary Accompaniments*

[F^V]

It is not enough to know what intervals accompany each [figured] interval; it is also necessary to mention what one must do on each interval [of the bass], ascending, or descending. One will learn this by means of the following rules, after having observed that on *Mi's* (A), *Si's* (B), and on sharped notes (C,D), one ordinarily plays the sixth.

[G^V]

Ex. 14

Rules for the Intervals[185]

When the bass ascends a semitone, a sixth is played on the first [bass] note, and a diminished fifth is played as a passing tone (A, B, C, D, E).

Ex. 15

When the bass ascends a minor third or descends a major sixth, a minor third is played on the first note (A). When the bass ascends a major third or descends a minor sixth, a major third is played on the first note (B,C).

Ex. 16

---

[185] In this section, Delair explains how to realize unfigured basses. The student is directed to memorize figures for two-note progressions, according to the intervallic motion of the bass.

When the bass ascends a fourth (A), or descends a fifth (B), a major third is played on the first note, and a minor seventh is played as a passing tone.

[H]

Ex. 17

A   B

When the bass ascends a fifth (A,C) or descends a fourth (B,D), a sixth is ordinarily played as a passing tone.

Ex. 18

A   B   C   D   E

When the bass descends a semitone (A,B), a tritone may be played as a passing tone on the end of the first note; a sixth is played on the second note.

Ex. 19

A   B

When the bass descends a tone, and when a seventh is not played on the second note, a major sixth is played on the first note.

[H^V]

Ex. 20

A   B

When the bass descends a minor third or ascends a major sixth, a minor third is played on the last note (A), and a major third on the first note (B). When the bass descends a major third or ascends a minor sixth, a major third is played on the last note (C,D).

Ex. 21

When the bass descends a diminished fourth (A,B), a sixth is played on the first note.

Ex. 22

I have included the chord progressions in the preceding examples, not only to show the normal resolutions of each chord, but also to accustom the player to accompanying in such a way that if he masters the rules and the preceding examples on all the notes, learning by rote as well as by reasoning, he will accompany at sight without difficulty.

[I]

One should not be surprised to find, later in the treatise, the same rules which I have introduced here in shortened form. At first, I had envisaged offering only the complete accompaniment treatise, but since then I have extracted the preceding summary. This contains the most basic precepts, to facilitate study by those who, having no knowledge of accompaniment, would be discouraged at first by the quantity of rules and observations which the treatise contains. These will be learned afterwards with much greater ease, [the beginner] having acquired a knowledge of the principles first.

General Rules which One Should Know
Before Accompanying[186]

   The natural chord can be called the fundamental chord, for which all the others are simply substitutions (*suppositions*); the fourth substitutes for the third, the sixth substitutes for the fifth, the seventh and the ninth substitute for the octave. Thus, to know [which intervals] accompany a [figured] interval that is not a part of the natural chord, one must observe what notes of the natural chord the interval replaces. Since the fourth takes the place of the third, it is accompanied by the fifth and the octave, the other notes of the natural chord. The sixth, which takes the place of the fifth, is accompanied naturally by the third and the octave; the ninth and the seventh, which take the place of the octave, are accompanied by the third and the fifth, the chord tones which should accompany the octave. The notes of the natural chord, and the chord tones which substitute for them are shown:

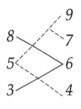

[J]

   The second, which we have not discussed, either as part of the natural chord, or as one of the intervals which can enter into the natural chord by substitution, is the natural chord of the note above the

---

[186]General Rules are from the 1724 edition.

principal. Thus, the second above *Ut* is the natural chord of *Re*. The tritone or augmented fourth, with the accompanying chord tones natural to it, forms the major chord of *Re*.

Sharped tones must ascend by conjunct degree, and flatted tones, as well as the fourth, the seventh and the ninth, must descend by conjunct degree.

When the bass ascends, the upper parts must descend or, if the chord above the preceding bass suits the following note, this chord must be sustained over both notes.

Ex. 23

When the bass descends, the other voices must ascend, or be sustained, for the reasons stated above.

Ex. 24

If the bass ascends or descends a fourth, the other voices may move in similar motion with the bass.

Ex. 25

It must be mentioned that, ordinarily, the parts above the bass ascend or descend by only a degree, as has been shown in the preceding example.

The natural chord is played only on the notes which establish the key of a piece. These are the last notes to which the bass either ascends or descends. The fourth, seventh, and ninth do not conflict with these notes.[187]

---

[187]By this Delair means that the fourth, seventh and ninth may substitute for the natural chord as "supposed" consonances.

Accidentals, or sharped notes, do not establish the key of a piece. It is the note one degree higher that establishes it, and on which the natural chord should be played. The sharped note is the leading tone, which means that the note above is the principal of the tone.

[K]

Since it is impossible to accompany well without having a knowledge of the notes which establish the key, one should work hard at [learning how to] distinguish these notes. This is one of the principal rules for accompanying figured or unfigured basses. These notes reveal the key and indicate where to play the natural chord, which is played only on the principal and dominant of the key, as will be seen by what follows.

When the bass ascends a degree to a note which establishes a key, a 6/5/3 is played on the first [bass] note. If the bass only ascends a semitone, the fifth which is played on the first note is diminished. This first [bass] note is the leading tone, and the second note is the principal (A), as has been stated above. When the bass ascends a tone, the fifth above the first [bass] note is perfect, and the second bass note is the dominant. The major chord [5/3] is played on the dominant when it establishes the key (B). When it does not, a 6/4 chord is played (C, D).

Ex. 26

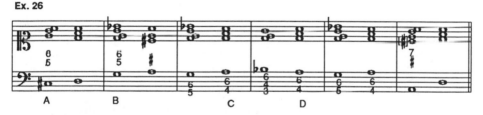

When the bass descends a degree to a note which establishes the key, a 6/4/3 chord is played on the first note. If the bass only descends a semitone, the fourth above the first bass note is augmented, and the second bass note is the dominant, on which a major chord is played (A). When the bass descends a tone, the second bass note is the principal (B). If the fourth has not been sounded in the preceding chord, it is not played with the sixth; an 8/6/3 chord is played instead (C).

Ex. 27

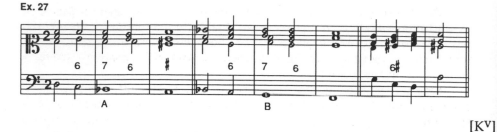

[K^V]

It is easy to ascertain the key, and where the natural chord should be played, by the notes which establish the key. Thus, I will not mention this anymore in the body of the treatise, and when I give rules for the different intervals of the bass which ascend or descend by third, fourth, fifth, etc., it should be understood that the last note establishes the key.

In *natural harmony*, the sixth is ordinarily played on all notes which do not establish the key.

When a note of the bass has just been or will be sharped or flatted, and this note enters into the realization, this note is sharped or flatted as in the bass. When a note which forms [the interval of] a fourth, a seventh, or a ninth [against the bass] has been flatted or sharped in the preceding chord, this note should be flatted or sharped accordingly (A,B,C).

Ex. 28

The sixth is played without the diminished fifth on notes that are [a semitone] below flatted notes (A), unless this note is the leading tone since, in this case, it would be necessary to play the diminished fifth (B).

Ex. 29

The minor third is ordinarily played on notes which are [a tone] above flatted notes (A), unless this third clashes with the mode (B).

Ex. 30   [L]

When the right hand is close to the left, and the bass is going to ascend considerably, one disengages the right hand on a note which requires the sixth, doubling the third. Then, when the bass is quite high, one omits the octave, playing only the third and fifth, and performing a *pincé* between the second and third.[188]

One can also bring the right hand closer to the left when the bass descends a great deal, by lowering the two hands on a note which requires the sixth, and playing only the third and sixth to avoid too large a distance between the two hands.

The octave can be added to all chords when it is hidden. It can be played, even if not, when the bass descends and the upper parts ascend (A).[189]

Ex. 31

A

The sixth is the most usual chord in natural harmony, since the natural chord is played only on notes which establish the key, as has been stated above, and the sixth is played on all the other notes. The sixth is accompanied variously, according to the interval of the bass, and according to the note of the scale on which the sixth occurs, when the key is fixed. One can have a clear understanding of the chord tones which accompany the sixth only by observing the different notes of the scale on which it is played.

We have spoken of the interval of an ascending or descending degree which establishes the key. Once one perceives that the key is established by this interval, one observes the essential pitches of the key in question. There are four essential notes in the major mode, at a distance of a third, one from the other.[190]

Ex. 32

---

[188]As the bass climbs, the player may bring the right hand up by pivoting on a sixth chord. Then, one reduces the texture to two notes in the right hand, enriching the sonority by adding a *pincé*, or mordent on the third of the chord.

[189]Delair is offering practical advice on how to avoid parallel octaves.

[190]This statement from the 1724 edition is in conflict with Delair's remark in the 1690 edition that there are only three essential pitches of the mode. See Chapter VII, "Rule for Knowing [the Key] of a Piece." The revision reflects developing ideas of tonal theory in the eighteenth century.

In the minor mode, one other essential note must be added--the [flatted] sixth of the key, which produces all the diminished chords, just as the leading tone produces all the augmented chords. We will speak in depth of the major and minor modes and the differences between them at the end of the treatise.

Within the compass of the natural octave, the natural chord is played only on the principal and the dominant, and the sixth, accompanied variously, is played on all the other [degrees of the scale]. On the second note of the key, a 6#/4/3 chord is played; on the mediant, 8/6/3; on the fourth, 6/5/3; on the sixth, 3/6/3; on the seventh, 6/5/3.

Ex. 33

In descending, the [bass] notes are, for the most part, accompanied differently. On the seventh degree, a 6/3 is played; on the sixth, a 6#/4/3; on the fourth, 6/4#/2. The last three notes are accompanied by the same chords as in ascending.

Ex. 34

It can be seen from the preceding rules that the octave [above the bass] is played on the principal, the mediant and the dominant. It can be played on other degrees if preceded or followed by another interval.[191] The octave is not a necessary interval when the bass proceeds by conjunct degree, because it has been played in the preceding chord and/or will be played in the following one. Thus, the octave is not played on the second degree of the key, because it has just been played on the principal; it is not played on the fourth, because it has just been played on the mediant, and will be played on the dominant. It is not played on the sixth, having just been played on the dominant; it is not played on the seventh, because it will be played on the principal. The same rule is observed in descending.

---

[191]To prevent parallel octaves, Delair advises the accompanist not to double the octave above the bass in consecutive chords.

The *rule of the octave* is not used when the bass proceeds by disjunct degree, when the key is not established, since then each note can establish the key.[192]

[M]

Ex. 35

This rule is also not used in *harmony by interval*, which uses just dissonances which may or may not follow one another; neither is it used in chromatic music which proceeds by semitones, nor in *extraordinary harmony*, which uses false dissonances. We will explain these different harmonies at the end of the treatise.

The *rule of the octave* does not determine the different accompaniments appropriate to [figured] intervals. This can only be determined by the *rule of the intervals*, which rule makes up the principal body of the treatise that follows. Thus, it is unreasonable that many people base all accompaniment on the *rule of the octave*, a rule comprising only the smallest part thereof.

There are as many keys as there are different notes in music. It is not sufficient to know the key; it is also necessary to be mindful of the mode, determined by the mediant of the key. If the mediant forms the major third above the principal, the key is sharp or major. If the mediant forms the minor third, the mode or key is minor. Only *Ut, Fa, Sol* and all the flatted notes in the bass are naturally major modes or keys. *Re, Mi, La, Si* and the sharped notes have the minor third naturally; consequently these modes are naturally minor or flat. Modes which are naturally minor can become major by means of a sharp one places after the clef on the position of the third, changing them from minor, their natural mode, to major. Modes naturally major can become minor by means of a flat one places on the position of the third [after the clef], changing them from major, their natural mode, to minor. In this manner, these sharps or flats change the species of the modes.

[M^V]

After having looked at key and mode, one must have a knowledge of *modulation*,[193] the differing configurations of the semitones within the octave. In a sharp or major key, in ascending, the semitones lie between the third and the fourth, and between the seventh and the octave. In descending, the semitones are found between the octave and the seventh,

---

[192]Delair refers to modulatory passages in which the bass moves by leap.
[193]The term *modulation* refers to the diatonic progression of pitches within the octave.

and between the fourth and the sharped third, going back by the same notes with which one has ascended.

In a flat or minor key, in ascending, the semitones are found between the second and the third, and between the seventh and the octave. In descending, they are found between the sixth and the fifth, and between the third and the second. This is the basis for the accidentals--sharps and flats--found in a given mode.

From this observation concerning the position of the semitones, one will know which notes should be sharped or flatted in any key or mode, when going up or down the octave.

These general rules, which can be applied to accompaniment consistently, should be thoroughly learned. [The few exceptions] to these rules will be seen at one's leisure later in the body of the treatise. It will be observed that a principal rule of accompaniment stipulates never to do anything that clashes with the mode. Exceptions which concern intervals [of the bass] increase as the different keys or modes reached, successively, increase. These keys or modes can be recognized by the notes that establish the key, and by those which terminate cadences. Exceptions concerning the interval of an ascending fourth are especially noticeable.[194] I will not point out the reasons since they can be easily deduced; in this way, one is required to reflect on the rules.

---

[194]i.e., if the piece modulates to foreign keys via the circle of fifths, the accompanist should take care that the realization incorporates the accidentals appropriate to the new keys.

TREATISE PROPER

I

Principles of Music It Is Necessary to Know for Accompanying

Before anything else, it is necessary to know the scale by memory, in ascending as well as descending order. The scale consists of seven degrees:

Ex. 36

$$E\ldots Si\ldots Mi$$
$$D\ldots La\ldots Re$$
$$C\ldots Sol\ldots Vt$$
$$B\ldots Fa\ldots Si$$
$$A\ldots Mi\ldots La$$
$$G\ldots Re\ldots Sol$$
$$F\ldots Vt\ldots Fa$$

en montant — *en deicendant*

The scale contains seven notes:

Ex. 37

$$Si$$
$$La$$
$$Sol$$
$$Fa$$
$$Mi$$
$$Re$$
$$Vt$$

en montant — *en deicendant*

It is also necessary to memorize these notes in succession, in ascending as well as descending order. To avoid the difficulty caused by the scale degrees, especially in solmization, from here on I will only use the names of the notes.[195]

[2]

One only needs to know which degree of the scale each note signifies. This is easily learned if one observes that the last note named in each degree is used to signify the whole degree. Thus, *Ut* signifies *C Sol Ut*; *Re* refers to *D La Re*, etc.

Assuming this, one can easily recognize the degrees of the scale by the notes. The degrees of the scale are used only when giving or taking the pitch on an instrument. This is because the different manners or methods the masters use to teach music can be standardized only by using the scale degrees.

Notes are named in order to distinguish different pitches. Thus, *Ut*, where custom would have us begin, is lower than *Re*; *Re* is lower than *Mi*, etc.

It is also necessary to observe that all successive notes are not at an equal distance one from the other, since some are a tone, and others a semitone, apart.

The notes that are a tone apart are those from *Ut* to *Re*, from *Re* to *Mi*, from *Fa* to *Sol*, from *Sol* to *La*, and from *La* to *Si*.

The notes that are a semitone apart are those from *Mi* to *Fa*, and from *Si* to *Ut*.

On [keyboard] instruments, the tone is distinguished from the semitone in that it takes three keys, inclusive, to make a tone, and two to make a semitone.

[3]

The natural order of the notes in relation to the tones and semitones is frequently changed, either by a flat made thus, *b*, which lowers by a semitone the notes to which it is attached, or that are found with it on the same line; or by a sharp made thus, #, which raises by a semitone the notes that follow immediately, or that are found on the same line. Thus, the natural tones become semitones by means of flats, and the natural semitones become tones by means of sharps.

---

[195]The hexachord system employed during the Middle Ages and Renaissance required that a note be called by its letter name and two solmization syllables according to its position within the soft and natural hexachords. The difficulties posed by this system, with mutation between natural, soft and hard hexachords, beginning on C, F, and G, respectively, caused it to be replaced by a "fixed-do" system in France in the late seventeenth century. For a discussion of the adoption of this new system, see Etienne Loulié, *Elements or Principles of Music*, trans. Albert Cohen (New York, 1965), pp. 43-44. Cited by Harris-Warrick, p. 10.

After [acquiring] a knowledge of the notes, one must learn the clefs.

A clef is placed at the beginning of each line. Clefs serve to establish certain notes on the lines or spaces, according to the kind or position of the clef. The three clefs are notated, and placed, as follows:

The clef of Ut, or C Sol Ut:

The clef of Fa, or F Ut Fa:

The clef of Sol, or G Re Sol:

The name for each of these clefs corresponds to the name one calls the note on the line or space where the clef is positioned. Thus, on the clef of *Ut*, one always says *Ut*; on that of *Fa*, one always says *Fa*; on that of *Sol*, one always says *Sol*, the notes always following the position of the clefs.[196]

In accompaniment, only the first two clefs are used, the clefs of *Ut* and *Fa*. This latter is the usual clef; the clef of *Ut* is rarely used, since it is only needed when the bass climbs extremely high, or when the alto takes the place of the bass.

The clef of *Fa* is ordinarily placed on the fourth line (A), and that of *Ut* on the third or middle line (B).

---

[196]In his example, Delair shows seven clefs. In modern terminology, the four C clefs are the soprano, mezzo-soprano, alto, and tenor clefs; the F clefs are the baritone and bass clefs; and the G clefs refer to the French violin and treble clefs, respectively. Saint Lambert objects to the use of multiple and movable clefs; his proposal to reduce the number of clefs, though not adopted, provoked some controversy in the eighteenth century. See Harris-Warrick, p. xiv.

Ex. 38: *Clefs of Fa and Ut*

This is not so fixed that one cannot change the position of the clefs. Often, one encounters the clef of Fa on the third line (A), and that of Ut on the second (B), or fourth line (C), especially in Italian music. The notes change according to the difference in the kind and position of the clefs.

Ex. 39: *Clefs of Fa and Ut*

II

Rules for Knowing the Notes by the Clefs

In order to know the notes of a piece, it is first necessary to observe the kind and position of the clef. On the line where the clef is located, imagine the note suitable to the clef, then count one note for each line and each space, ascending or descending, always following the natural order of the notes, until the desired note is reached. Thus, on the clef of *Fa*, one will count, in descending: *Fa, Mi, Re, Ut*, etc., placing one note on each line and in each space, as we have just said. On the clef of Ut, one will count, in ascending, beginning with the name of the clef: *Ut, Re, Mi, Fa*; and in descending, *Ut, Si, La, Sol*, etc.

There is a great deal of difference between vocal and instrumental music, the latter being easier than the former, since, in it, one does not change the names of the notes even when sharps or flats are encountered immediately after the clef.[197] This saves great difficulty--a difficulty which cannot be avoided in vocal music.

When flats are encountered after the clef, it is necessary to lower by a semitone the notes situated on the lines or spaces where these flats are placed. When sharps are encountered, it is necessary to raise by a semitone the notes that are found on the lines or spaces where the sharps are situated.

---

[197]Delair refers to the process of mutation in solmization, which requires modulation between natural, soft and hard hexachords, and thus a changing of solmization syllables depending on the hexachord encompassed by the key.

The natural, which is made thus, ♮, suppresses the preceding flat, restoring the following note to its natural state.

After learning the notes on paper, it is necessary to acquire a knowledge of the notes on the instrument one wishes to use for accompanying.

[5]

Not every instrument is suitable for accompanying, since, in accompaniment, the trebles should not dominate the basses. It is out of the question to allow the instrument to stand out when accompanying; rather, one should only support the voice which one accompanies. Thus, it is necessary that the basses dominate. This is the reason one ordinarily does not use the lute or guitar to accompany, since the trebles are too dominant and the basses not loud enough.

Ordinarily, one accompanies chordally only on the theorbo or the harpsichord; thus, it is sufficient to explain the notes and the clefs on these two instruments.

Rules for Knowing the Clefs and the Notes on the Theorbo

There are fourteen strings on the theorbo; the first six are called the *petit jeu*, since they are but half as long as the other eight. The latter serve only for the basses.

It is impossible to determine the notes on the theorbo by the music alone, since there are several strings which, making a unison together, can be distinguished only by a tablature, which consists of the letters: "a, b, c, d, e, f, g, h, i, k, l."

The letter "a" indicates the strings played with only the right hand; the left hand does nothing on these strings.

The other letters indicate the sequence of frets on the neck: "b" indicates the first fret on top, "c" the second, "d" the third, etc.

[6]

This tablature is used only for the *petit jeu*, which contains the first six strings, expressed by six lines. On the eight others that follow, the left hand does not do anything, since these strings are played only with the right thumb. They are indicated by "a's" under the six lines, and are differentiated by the number of little bars that precede them, or by numbers placed underneath the six lines. It is assumed that one always adds seven to the number of bars or numbers encountered underneath these lines. Thus, "a" alone under the six lines indicates the seventh string, "a" preceded by a bar indicates the eighth, . . . until the fourteenth string.

Although the bars and the numbers do the same thing, one uses the numbers when four or five are exceeded, because one could easily make a mistake in counting six or seven bars all at once, whereas a number can be seen at first sight.

Ex. 40: *Succession of Bass Notes on the Theorbo*

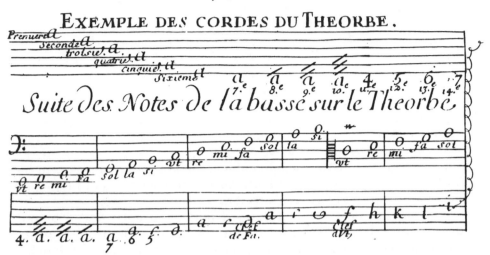

The numbers beneath *Sol, La,* and *Si* indicate notes which cannot be notated on the staff because their range is too low. They serve only to fill out [the sonority]; this is the reason I have included them beneath their octaves.

The clef of *F Ut Fa* is taken on "*d*" on the fifth line, and that of *C Sol Ut* is taken on "*f*" on the fourth line. The theorbo does not have a range that is high enough to supply the compass needed for the treble clefs. One makes up for this defect by taking the treble notes an octave lower.

In music, two clefs are used for the treble: the clef of *Ut* on the first line, and that of *Sol* on the first and second lines.[198]

Ex. 41: *Treble Clefs*

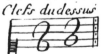

[7]

The following will demonstrate the position of the treble clefs, and the treble range of the theorbo.[199]

---

[198]i.e., soprano, French violin and treble clefs.

[199]Delair shows the notes c' to a" on the five-line staff. Underneath he gives their equivalents in lute tablature, transposed down by one or two octaves, since these notes exceed the treble range of the theorbo.

Ex. 42:: *Succession of Treble Notes on the Theorbo*

Knowledge of the treble clefs is necessary for taking or giving the pitch of the piece one wishes to accompany, and a knowledge of the compass of the theorbo in the upper register is necessary for finding all the notes which comprise the chords above the bass.

For a greater understanding of the notes on the theorbo, one will see in the following, in shortened form, all the possible ways of finding all the notes--natural as well as sharped and flatted.

It must be observed that sharped notes, and notes flatted by one degree above these sharped notes, are the same pitch on instruments, although they differ in notation, as one will see by the following example: [200]

Ex. 43: *Theorbo Tablature*

This summary of notes will greatly facilitate accompaniment. Since all intervals are composed of these notes, they can be found easily by using the preceding table. The table can also be used for finding the accompaniments [to these figured intervals], which will then fall more readily under the hand.

---

[200]In this example, Delair gives the enharmonic equivalents of each note of the octave, along with the various ways they can be played on the theorbo, on different strings and in different octaves.

When there is a sharp or flat at the beginning of a piece, it is necessary to lower or raise by a semitone the notes of the bass which are found in the position of these flats or sharps.

[8]

After learning the notes, and before proceeding to the rules that deal with the chords used in accompaniment, it is useful to practice playing the basses alone with the thumb of the right hand on the strings reserved for the bass notes, not surpassing the fourth string, until one can find all the notes easily. Then one should play the upper parts alone on the first three strings, using the first two fingers of the right hand alternately for plucking the strings, holding the little finger pressed to the fingerboard to keep the hand in position. Then, one may proceed to a knowledge of chords and meter. An understanding of the latter is necessary to determine note values, and to give a suitable movement[201] to pieces. However, since these things concern accompaniment in general on any instrument, we will discuss them after having given the principles necessary for accompanying on the harpsichord.

Rules for Knowing the Clefs and the Notes on the Harpsichord

The harpsichord is an instrument that is much easier and more practical than the theorbo, since the hand works much less on the harpsichord, and the eyes lead directly to the notes and chords which one needs.

There are two kinds of keys on the harpsichord: the flat [lower] keys, called naturals, which express the natural notes, and those which are found [raised] between the naturals, which express the sharped and flatted notes. These are commonly called accidentals.

Ordinary harpsichords contain fifty or fifty-one keys, of which the second accidental from the bottom is split. The keys are a semitone apart, except for the first five or six, which do not follow this order, since they have neither flat nor sharp keys.[202] All the others have their sharp or flat, except those which are found between the sharp of the note which precedes them and the flat of the note which follows, since these notes cannot have either one naturally.

[9]

---

[201]The term *mouvement* refers to the expression as well as the tempo.

[202]Delair authenticates that the most usual harpsichord in late seventeenth-century France was a "short-octave" instrument, with the range GG (apparent BB) to c'''. The instrument is tuned such that the lowest key, BB, actually sounds GG; "apparent" C-sharp sounds AA, and the key E-Flat is split to accommodate both BB and E-flat. After C and D the keys are tuned chromatically.

To find the notes on the harpsichord, notice that the first key at the bottom is a *Sol*. *La* and *Si* are found on the first and second accidentals, with *Ut*, *Re* and *Mi* on the second, third and fourth natural [keys]. After this, all the notes follow one another chromatically until the fifth *Ut* at the top, the last note of the harpsichord. There are some extraordinary harpsichords containing fifty-three keys, which begin and finish with the same notes as ordinary harpsichords. On these harpsichords all the notes follow each other naturally with their sharps and flats.

The clef of *F Ut Fa* begins on the second *Fa*, the clef of *C Sol Ut*, on the third *Ut*, and that of *G Re Sol*, on the fourth *Sol*.

By knowing the clefs, one can find the position of the notes in such a way that, when the notes are above the clefs, one counts, in ascending, one note on each line and on each space, always beginning with the position of the clef, until the desired note is reached. The same order is followed in descending.

On the clef of *F Ut Fa*, one will count, in ascending, *Fa, Sol, La,* and, in descending, *Fa, Mi, Re,* etc.

On the clef of *C Sol Ut*, one will count, in ascending, *Ut, Re, Mi,* and, in descending, *Ut, Si, La*; on the clef of *G Re Sol*, one will count, in ascending, *Sol, La, Si,* and, in descending, *Sol, Fa, Mi,* always following the order of the notes, whether ascending or descending, as has been said above.

Although the treble clefs are not used for [notating basses in] accompaniment, it is necessary to know them, nonetheless, in order to give or take the pitch of that which one accompanies.

If one or more flats are encountered at the beginning of the clef, it is necessary to sound all the notes found on the lines or spaces of these flats, on the accidentals that are below the natural notes. For example, if there is a flat on the line of *Si*, it is necessary to sound the accidental that is below *Si* natural. If the flat is on *Mi*, it is necessary to sound the accidental that is below *Mi* natural. It is the same for the others.

[10]

When a sharp is found immediately after the clef, it is necessary to play the notes that are encountered on the lines and spaces of these sharps, on the accidentals above the natural notes. For example, if there is a sharp on *Ut*, it is necessary to play the accidental above *Ut*. If there is a sharp on *Fa*, it is necessary to play the accidental above *Fa*.

In vocal music, the sharp and the natural have the same property, but on the harpsichord, they differ in that the sharp is ordinarily played on the accidental keys, and the natural on the natural keys. The reason for this is that the sharps raise the notes by a semitone above their "nature," and the natural restores them to their "nature," merely suppressing the flat that preceded them.

The flats or sharps encountered in the course of a piece affect only the notes that immediately follow them.

Not all notes can be sharped or flatted naturally, since there are some that are found between the sharp of the preceding note and the flat of the following note and, thus, cannot have either one naturally. Such are the *Re* and the *La*.[203] Nevertheless, by means of transpositions not formerly known, but which are very much in use now, one may sharpen and flatten all the notes. This can be observed in the double circle which follows. One will see in the first circle, the one closest to the center, the sequence of natural notes and those notes that can be sharped and flatted naturally. In the second circle, one will see the notes that are sharped and flatted by transposition.

In general musical terms, a piece is called transposed if, by means of sharps and flats, it is higher or lower than it should be naturally, thereby altering the natural order of the notes in relation to the tones and semitones.[204]

[11]

Ex. 44: *Circle of Natural and Transposed Notes*

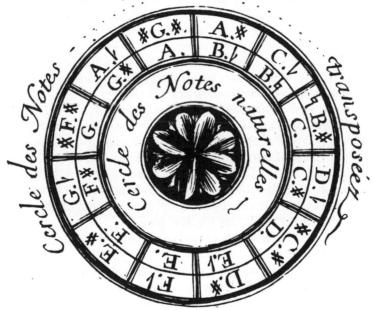

---

[203]*Re* and *La* cannot be sharped or flatted, for reasons of tuning. In meantone temperament, Db is tuned to C# and D# is tuned to Eb. Similarly, G# is tuned to Ab and A# to Bb. Saint Lambert makes the same distinction. See Harris-Warrick, p. 19.

[204]Here, Delair uses the term transposition the way we use it today, i.e. the rewriting or performance of a piece in a different key. In Chapter VII, "Rules for Transpositions," Delair discusses transposition in the context of modal theory.

The notes belonging to the keyboard of the harpsichord are contained in the first circle. One will observe that the keyboard contains only twelve different keys, each producing a different pitch. As I have already said, the keys differ successively by a semitone. It follows from this that, on the harpsichord as well as in all of music, there are only twelve pitches, the twelve semitones, which comprise the compass of an octave in which all music is contained. All other possible semitones are but replicas of these. This is perfectly well expressed by this circle, in which the end of one octave leads to the beginning of another, to infinity.

In this circle,[205] I use the degrees of the scale, indicated by the letters with which they begin. For example, F signifies *F Ut Fa*, G indicates *G Re Sol*, and so forth.

Frequently, two letters signify the same degree, but nevertheless differ by a semitone. This is indicated by a sharp or natural, which raises the degree by a semitone, or by a flat, which lowers the degree by a semitone.

[12]

Each degree of the scale can be varied in three or four ways, since it is either natural, flatted, sharped, or even sometimes double sharped, as can be seen at *C Sol Ut*, at *F Ut Fa*, and at *G Re Sol* in the second circle. These double sharped degrees serve for transposition, and to supply the notes for possible intervals, as will be observed below.

I know that these double sharped notes will look like a new invention to those who have not thoroughly examined the rules of transpositions, but I would argue that one should not be more surprised to see these notes double sharped than to encounter sharps on *Mi's*, *Si's*, and *La's*, which, being naturally sharped, are nevertheless sharped again. *Ut*, *Fa* and *Sol* sharped at the beginning of the clef, in transposed major keys, take the place of *Mi*, *Si*, and *La*. Thus, in the course of a piece, these notes can be sharped again, just as easily as can *Mi*, *Si* and *La*. I admit that this is rare, but it is sometimes encountered. I have a printed Italian piece in which there is a *Re* sharp with the major third marked above it, which should be *Fa*, double sharped.

One will see the usefulness of these double sharped notes in distinguishing intervals.

It can be seen in the above circle that each key of the harpsichord has two different names, of which one is natural to it, and the other is transposed. The natural names are in the first circle, and the transposed names are in the second.

---

[205]With his *Circle of Natural and Transposed Notes*, Delair becomes one of the first theorists to set forth the concept of enharmonic equivalence.

There are harpsichords in which the keys are split, so that each note, whether natural or transposed, has its own particular key. However, these instruments are not used because of the difficulty in playing them.[206] Here is what can be said toward an understanding of clefs, the notes, and the transpositions on the harpsichord. Let us proceed to the rules of accompaniment, beginning with a knowledge of chords.

---

[206]The harpsichord to which Delair refers has a fully chromatic keyboard and split keys for each accidental. In a meantone temperament, the usual tuning of keyboards in the seventeenth-century, the only available chromatic notes are C#, Eb, F#, G# and Bb. Since enharmonics are not possible in the twelve-note scale (G# cannot serve as Ab, nor D# as Eb, for example), it is evident that the range of harmonic modulation is restricted. Hence, the key of B major is unusable since Eb is tuned as a pure interval to G, making the third between B and D#/Eb inordinately wide and out of tune. The use of split-key accidentals as a solution to this problem was prevalent in Spain, Italy and Germany. Moreover, experimentation with chromatic and enharmonic *genera* in seventeenth-century music led to the design of some unusual split-keyed instruments. Vito Trasuntino, an early seventeenth-century maker, built an *archicembalo* of four octaves from C, with each accidental divided into four keys, and an extra key divided in two parts between each of the natural key semitones, yielding thirty-notes to the octave. (Russell, p. 32). In France, Mersenne tells us that Jehan Titelouze owned a harpsichord with nineteen-notes to the octave. (Mersenne, *Harmonie Universelle*, vol. II, pp. 438-39). Delair makes reference to the difficulty in playing these instruments; apparently they were purely experimental.

III

Principles of Composition which Serve as a Foundation for Accompaniment in General, On All Kinds of Instruments

I will use the word chord to express all the different intervals which sound together, whether they produce accord or discord.[207]

[13]

A chord is the meeting of different pitches sounding together. These pitches form semitones and tones, which in turn form intervals, and intervals form chords. Therefore, chords are composed of pitches, semitones, tones, and intervals. This is why, before going further, it is necessary to know what pitch, semitone, tone, and interval are. Afterwards, we will proceed to a knowledge of chords, which are composed of all of these, and then we will treat in depth the rules of accompaniment, showing which chords one is obliged to play above each interval [of the bass].[208]

Concerning Pitch

A pitch is a sound expressed alone by a voice or an instrument, without modulation. Pitch is the very foundation of music, since music is composed only of pitches.

---

[207]The use of the term *accord* to mean consonance is seen in other contemporary French writings, including those by Brossard and Saint Lambert.
[208]Delair refers to the harmonization of unfigured basses according to the intervallic motion of the bass.

Concerning the Semitone

The semitone is composed of two consecutive pitches. There are two kinds of semitones, minor and major.[209] The minor semitone contains two different pitches of the same name, as from *Fa* natural to *Fa* sharp, or from *Mi* flat to *Mi* natural.

Ex. 45

The major semitone contains two successive pitches of different names, such as *Si, Ut* and *Mi, Fa.*

Ex. 46

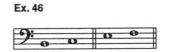

There is a clear difference between the major and minor semitones, such that the voice distinguishes them perfectly, making the interval from *Ut* natural to *Ut* sharp smaller than that from *Ut* sharp to *Re*, although on instruments the semitones are not differentiated.[210]

[14]

Concerning the Tone

The tone is composed of two semitones of different species, a minor and a major, like *Ut, Re* or *Re, Mi.* From *Ut* to *Ut* sharp, the semitone is minor, and from *Ut* sharp to *Re*, it is major; from *Re* to *Mi* flat, the semitone is major, and from *Mi* flat to *Mi* natural, the semitone is minor. It is the same for all the tones.

Ex. 47

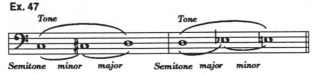

[209]Under the entry, "Seconda," Brossard explains that the tone may be divided into two unequal semitones. The major semitone contains 5 commas, and the minor semitone 4 commas. (Brossard, *Dictionnaire*, pp. 101-102).

[210]Delair refers to just intonation, in which the diatonic and chromatic semitones are different sizes. Such differentiation is not possible on instruments since in equal temperament, which was used for tuning the theorbo, all semitones are equal. In a meantone temperament--the tempering system used for keyboard instruments--the semitones are of different sizes, but enharmonic tones are not possible. For a discussion of lute temperaments, see Mark Lindley, *Lutes, Viols, and Temperaments* (Cambridge: Cambridge University Press, 1984).

Concerning Intervals

The intervals are composed of semitones, tones, or both.

There are seven principal [melodic] intervals: that is to say, the second, the third, the fourth, the fifth, the sixth, the seventh, and the octave. These are differentiated by the number of notes or degrees they contain. The interval of a second is called thus because it contains two degrees; the interval of a third contains three, as with the others.

All the other possible intervals relate to these, being but replicas of them. For example, the interval of a ninth corresponds to the interval of a second, that of a tenth to that of a third, and so forth.

Ex. 48

Example of Intervals and Their Replicas

Replicas of a second third fourth

Interval of a   tone   third   fourth   fifth   sixth   seventh octave   ninth   tenth   eleventh
semitone

Concerning Chords in General

Chords are composed of intervals. A chord (*accord*) is the meeting of a low pitch with a high one. When sung together, they produce harmony, which is called chord.

[15]

By low pitch is meant the bass, or whatever takes its place, and by high pitch is meant the entire upper part, such as it is. Interval differs from chord, in that the first serves only for melody, which consists of the melodic line of one part alone, the line being composed only of consecutive intervals, while chord is found only in harmony, and results from the combination of several assembled parts.[211]

Like the seven [melodic] intervals, there are seven principal [harmonic] intervals: the second, the third, the fourth, the fifth, the sixth, the seventh, and the octave. The other intervals are only replicas of these: the ninth corresponds to the second, the tenth to the third, etc.

---

[211]Delair is one of the first theorists to differentiate between *intervalle* and *accord*, the former meaning consecutive pitches, or melodic interval, and the latter meaning two or more simultaneous pitches. When Delair uses *accord* to mean two simultaneous pitches, the term has been translated as "interval." In Chapter IV, "The Manner in Which to Mark Chords on the Continuo Basses," Delair makes a distinction between *accord* in composition, a harmonic interval above the bass, and *accord* in accompaniment, the chordal realization of that interval. While Delair seems to be referring here to *accord* in accompaniment, what we call chord, the subsequent discussion clearly concerns *accord* in composition, which has been translated in this context as harmonic interval or simply, interval.

To find a harmonic interval above the bass, it is necessary to count in ascending and not in descending. To find the third of *Ut*, one must count *Ut, Re, Mi* and not *Ut, Si, La*, etc.

Each interval takes its name from the number of notes or degrees it encompasses. The second is so-called because it contains two degrees, the third draws its name from the three degrees it contains, etc.

Ex. 49

| second | third | fourth | fifth | sixth | seventh | octave | Replicas: tenth eleventh ninth or third or fourth or second |

The intervals are divided into perfect and imperfect intervals.

A perfect interval is not subject to augmentation or diminution; such intervals are the fourth, the fifth and the octave. These intervals are fixed in size, since they are neither major nor minor, and cannot be augmented or diminished naturally.

An imperfect interval is subject to augmentation or diminution; such are the second, the third, the sixth, and the seventh. These intervals are sometimes minor and sometimes major, naturally or artificially. They can be augmented or diminished by applying sharps or flats, according to what is suitable.

All intervals, perfect as well as imperfect, can be divided into consonances, dissonances, and a mixture of the two.

[16]

A consonance is an interval that is good in itself, such as the third, the fifth, the sixth and the octave. A dissonance is an interval that is not good in itself; however, it is still used if preceded and followed by consonances suitable to it.

There are two kinds of dissonances, the just and the false.

The just dissonances are the second, the fourth, the seventh, and the ninth.

Although the second and the ninth are identical in nature, they are nonetheless different in their accompaniments, as we will see by what follows. That is why I have made a distinction between them.

The false dissonances are the augmented second, fourth and fifth, and the diminished fourth, fifth and seventh.

Today, we use many intervals that were not formerly employed.[212] To learn which intervals, both ordinary and extraordinary, are normally used by the experts, I will introduce in the ensuing treatise only those

---

[212]Delair documents the increasing use of chromatic intervals by French composers in the late seventeenth century.

which are current in French as well as in Italian music. It will be easy to distinguish those intervals that are not employed by knowing those that are.

I divide the seven principal intervals--the second, the third, the fourth, the fifth, the sixth, the seventh, and the octave--into seventeen usable intervals or chords. These are the minor second, the major second, the augmented second, the minor third, the major third, the natural fourth, the diminished fourth, the augmented fourth, the natural fifth, the diminished fifth, the augmented fifth, the minor sixth, the major sixth, the minor seventh, the major seventh, the diminished seventh, and the octave.

Rules for Recognizing and Distinguishing the Major and Minor Intervals

The minor second is composed of a semitone.

Ex. 50

When I speak simply of a semitone, I always mean the major semitone.

The major second is composed of one tone.

Ex. 51

[17]

Although the major second is composed of two diatonic notes, this does not mean it contains two tones, because the principal or first note of each interval is not counted, producing only a pitch and not a tone. For there to be a tone, there must be gradation from one pitch to another. Thus, the unison is not an interval, since an interval should contain one or more degrees. Nevertheless, it is tolerated in accompaniment on instruments which do not have octaves on all the notes, such as the theorbo. Then the unison may take the place of the octave.

The augmented second is composed of a tone and a minor semitone.

Ex. 52

The minor third contains a tone and a semitone.

Ex. 53

The major third contains two tones.

Ex. 54

The natural fourth contains two tones and a semitone.

Ex. 55

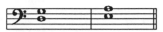

The augmented fourth is composed of three tones; this is why it is called a tritone.

Ex. 56

The diminished fourth contains a tone and two semitones.

Ex. 57

The natural fifth contains three tones and a semitone.

Ex. 58

The diminished or false fifth contains two tones and two semitones.

Ex. 59

The augmented fifth contains four tones.

Ex. 60

The minor sixth contains three tones and two semitones.

Ex. 61

The major sixth contains four tones and a semitone.

Ex. 62

[18]

The minor seventh contains four tones and two semitones.

Ex. 63

The major seventh contains five tones and a semitone.

Ex. 64

The diminished seventh contains three tones and three semitones.

Ex. 65

The octave contains five tones and two semitones.

Ex. 66

The octave is the only interval that should never undergo augmentation or diminution, although some people, by caprice rather than by reason, sometimes use it as augmented or diminished. This practice should be absolutely forbidden, for this interval can only produce a bad effect, especially when used against the bass. The augmented or diminished octave is also strictly prohibited between parts. For example, when a part produces a minor third or a minor sixth with the bass, one should never play a major third or major sixth simultaneously [in another part]. Those who make use of this interval use it in passing very lightly on the last part of a note. Thus, this interval is never marked in the accompaniment, because it does not carry [a chord]; that is why I do not show it among the number of intervals.

To remember the number of tones and semitones which are contained in each interval easily, notice that the intervals, minor as well as major, or of different species, differ successively by a semitone.

When going from a minor to a major interval of the same species, it is necessary to join the two semitones to make a tone, and when going from one interval to another of a different species, it is necessary to separate the semitones. This will be observed in the musical dial, which shows not only the number of tones and semitones which comprise the intervals commonly used, but also all possible intervals on any note, natural or transposed.

To use the dial, it is necessary to turn the needle at the center to the degree of the scale above which one wishes to find an interval.

[19]

The twelve lines in the middle of this dial lead to the degrees of the scale comprising the intervals designated on these lines. The intervals marked on the dial differ successively one from the other by a semitone, with this distinction: that minor and major intervals of the same species differ only by a minor semitone, while intervals of a different species differ by a major semitone.

See Ex. 67: *Dial of the Intervals*

Each line leads to two different [enharmonic] intervals which, if they are possible, are found in the first and second circles, respectively. To distinguish between an interval and its [enharmonic equivalent], one merely has to notice the number of degrees each interval contains.

I have said that one would find all the possible intervals by means of this dial. [What may appear to be omissions are not], since there are notes which do not have all the diminished or augmented intervals that others have--the natural as well as transposed notes having only those intervals, perfect and imperfect, that are natural to them.[213]

---

[213]Since Delair allows no double flats, and only three double sharps--C##, F## and G##--whether or not a particular interval can be formed above a given note depends on its position within the octave, i.e., the configuration of the semitones and tones around it. For example, Ut lacks the diminished third because E-flat cannot be double flatted. La has the diminished third because the minor third, C, falls on a natural note and thus can be flatted.

Ex. 67: *Dial of the Intervals*

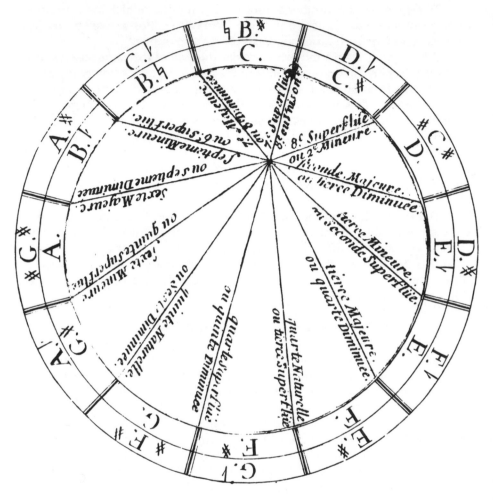

[20]

Only *Mi*, expressed by *E Si Mi*, and *La*, expressed by *A Mi La*, have all possible intervals.[214] The other notes are lacking in some interval, either diminished or augmented.

Ut natural lacks the diminished third, sixth, and seventh.

Ut sharp lacks the augmented second, third, and sixth.

Re has no diminished sixth.

Mi flat does not have any diminished intervals.

---

[214]Delair refers to the notes found in the inner circle of his dial. These correspond to the keys of a harpsichord tuned in meantone temperament.

Fa does not have the diminished third, fourth, sixth and seventh.

Fa sharp has neither the augmented third, nor the augmented sixth.

Sol has neither the diminished third, nor the diminished sixth.

Sol sharp lacks the augmented second, third, fifth, and sixth.

Si flat lacks the diminished third, fourth, sixth, seventh and octave.

Si natural has no augmented third.

The sharped notes of the second circle do not have any augmented intervals except *Re* sharp, which has the augmented fourth. Most lack several major intervals.

Ut sharp, of the second circle, lacks the major second, third, sixth, and seventh.

Re sharp does not lack any major interval.

Mi sharp has no major seventh.

Fa sharp has no major third, sixth, or seventh.

Sol sharp lacks the natural fifth and the major second, third, sixth, and seventh.

La sharp has all the major intervals.

Si sharp lacks the major third and major seventh.

The flatted notes of the second circle do not have any diminished intervals, and they lack several minor intervals.

Ut flat lacks the minor second, third, sixth, and seventh.

Re flat has neither the minor second, nor the minor sixth.

Fa flat lacks the minor second, third, sixth, and seventh, and even has no natural fourth.

Sol flat lacks the minor second, third, and sixth.

La flat lacks the minor second.

[21]

All the natural notes have their natural intervals in the first circle. One cannot, in any event, supply intervals not found in the two circles, since these circles contain the notes the farthest transposed that can still be used; thus, one can add nothing.

IV

The Manner in which to Mark Chords
on the Continuo Basses

A two indicates the second; a three indicates the third, etc.

Ex. 68

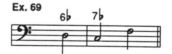

A flat after a figure indicates that the interval signified by the number should be minor. For example, a six and a flat indicate the minor sixth.

Ex. 69

A sharp after a figure indicates that the interval signified by the figure should be major. Thus, a six and a sharp indicate the major sixth.

Ex. 70

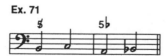

When there is neither a sharp nor a flat after the figures, it is necessary to make them natural.

The diminished fifth is frequently indicated by a slashed fifth, as well as by a five and a flat.

Ex. 71

Sharps or flats, which render intervals major or minor, are sometimes placed before or above the figures. This usage, which is frequent in Italian music, conforms to the usual rule in music that sharps and flats be placed before the notes they alter; however, in French operas, the sharps and flats are put after the numbers.[215]

Such usage is consistent with the manner of naming intervals, since one names the effects of flats or sharps, only after having named the intervals.[216] For example, one calls a flatted sixth a minor sixth, and a sharped sixth a major sixth. It makes no difference whether one puts the sharps or flats before or after the figures, or above or below the basses.

Sometimes, in opera scores, one finds a flat or a sharp before a figure. These flats or sharps do not affect these figures, but only indicate that one must make the natural chord major or minor, according to what is marked in front of these figures.

[22]

Ex. 72

Diminished intervals, like minor intervals, are indicated by a flat, and augmented intervals, like major intervals, by a sharp. These intervals cannot be sharped or flatted naturally above the bass notes on which they are marked without becoming diminished or augmented. Thus, flats and sharps render these chords diminished or augmented.

Augmented intervals are formed only on semitones and diminished intervals are formed on natural [keys], as one will see in the following example.[217]

Ex. 73

---

[215]In the opera scores of Jean-Baptiste Lully, the sharps and flats are consistently placed after the figures.

[216]Delair refers to the fact that, in French, the adjective (*bémolizée* or *diézée*) follows the noun (*sexte*) it modifies, just as the accidental follows the figure it alters in the figured basses of French opera scores.

[217]Delair clarifies this paragraph in the 1724 edition. The revision reads: "Augmented intervals are made only on notes that take major intervals naturally, and diminished intervals on those that take minor intervals. These intervals are used only in the minor mode."

A single flat on a note indicates the minor third (A).
A single sharp on a note indicates the major third (B).

Ex. 74

A   B

Flats or sharps are sometimes found with figures. They are [placed] below the figures and indicate that it is necessary to play the minor or major third with the intervals marked above them.

Ex. 75

It is necessary to distinguish flats and sharps found next to bass notes from those found above or below the bass. In the first case, the bass notes are raised or lowered a semitone, while, in the latter case, the chord is rendered major or minor.

The difference between a chord in composition and a chord in accompaniment is that the former signifies only a single note above the bass, while the latter includes the [additional] notes which accompany that note [to complete the chord].[218]   For example, the sixth, in composition, signifies simply the sixth. The sixth, in accompaniment, on the other hand, contains not only the [figured interval of a] sixth, but also the intervals that must accompany it.

Ordinary   Accompaniments

[23]

The most basic chord is the natural chord, which consists of the third, the fifth and the octave. It is possible to omit the octave--the third and the fifth being a sufficient accompaniment--especially when accompanying on the theorbo, an instrument on which finding the chords may be difficult, particularly in transposed pieces and those in a quick tempo.

I call it "natural chord" because it is composed of the most natural consonances.

---

[218]Delair makes a distinction between *accord* in composition, a harmonic interval above the bass, and *accord* in accompaniment, the chordal realization of that interval. These terms have been translated as interval and chord, respectively.

It is wrong to call this chord "perfect"[219] since the third often changes, being sometimes major and sometimes minor. The term natural is more appropriate since this chord contains the pitches which are essentially natural to its root. For example, the natural chord of *Ut* is composed of *Mi, Sol, Ut,* the essential pitches of *Ut.* The natural chord of *Re* is composed of *Fa, La, Re,* the essential pitches of *Re,* etc.

The natural chord is encountered in six different notations; that is, when there is nothing marked on a note, when there is a single three, or a single five, or a single eight, or when there is a sharp or a flat--the difference being that the third of the chord is major when there is a sharp, and minor when there is a flat.

Ex. 76

It must be noted that the "three," the "five," and the "eight" merely signify the natural chord, which is also played when there is nothing marked. It is useless to give the figures, except on those notes where one plays the natural chord on only a part of the notes: Thus, the third is marked only before or after the fourth; the fifth is marked before or after the sixth, or on an unfigured note that naturally takes the sixth; and the eighth is marked after the ninth.

Ex. 77

One always plays the natural chord with the natural third on the first note of the bass, no matter what follows, unless it [the bass] begins with a note that is a fifth higher or a fourth lower than the principal or final of the piece. [If this is the case, a major third must be played]. For example, when a piece whose final is *Sol* begins with *Re,* a major third must be played on the first note; if the final is *La* and the first note is *Mi,* a major third must be played on *Mi,* even though it is the first note.

[24]

Ex. 78

---

[219]See Glossary for a discussion of this term.

When I speak of the natural third I do not mean only thirds encountered naturally on each note, according to the tones or semitones that make up the thirds; I refer as well to thirds that are natural to the mode of the piece being accompanied. Frequently, there are encountered one or more flats after the clef which change the thirds that were naturally major into minor, or one or more sharps which change the thirds that were naturally minor into major. When there are accidentals, one must conform to them, and play, during the course of the piece, the thirds which they designate.

When there are flats or sharps at the beginning of the clefs, these sharps or flats affect those chords which contain the sharped or flatted notes, rendering them major or minor. For example, if *Fa* is sharped at the beginning of the clef, all the chords containing *Fa* should be major. If *Si* is flatted at the beginning, all the chords containing *Si* should be minor, as with the others.

The second is used in two different ways, since it is made either on the first or the second part of a bass note.

When it is made on the first part of a note, it is called a ninth (A), and when it is made on the second part, it is called a second (B).

Ex. 79

The second, marked on the second part of a syncopation,[220] should always be major. It is accompanied by a fourth, with which one plays either a fifth or a sixth. The sixth which accompanies the second should be of the same species as the third which precedes it on the first part of the note. Thus, if one has played a minor third before the second, the sixth which accompanies this second should also be minor (A), and if one has played a major third, the sixth should be major (B).

Ex. 80   [25]

It should be mentioned that, formerly, composers ordinarily played the fifth with the second instead of playing the sixth, as one can see in

---

[220]Bass suspension

the work of Eustache du Caurroy[221] and other skilled composers. Nevertheless, in opera choruses, one always encounters the sixth. It is true that when a minor third precedes the second, the sixth is a more harmonious accompaniment to the second than is the fifth; however, when a major third precedes it, the fifth is a more harmonious accompaniment than is the sixth. Thus, when accompanying only two or three voices, one may play the fifth with the second, principally when a major third precedes it. However, when accompanying a chorus, one plays the sixth. One can also double the second or fourth, instead of [playing] the sixth.[222]

When the second is marked on the first part of a bass note, whether major or minor, it is called a ninth. We will discuss this interval in its turn.

The figures I have included under the notes in the examples indicate the intervals that must be played, even in the absence of figures.

Italian composers use the augmented second;[223] it is accompanied by the tritone and the sixth.

Ex. 81

The fourth, preceded by a third on the same note, is accompanied by the sixth and the octave (A,B).

Ex. 82

---

[221] François Eustache du Caurroy (1549-1601) was a popular composer whose choral and instrumental works Delair considered out of date. Appointed *surintendant de la musique* under Henry IV, he achieved wide recognition in French musical circles. According to Mersenne, writing in 1636, "Du Caurroy reigns supreme for the great harmoniousness of his composition and his rich counterpoint . . . all the composers of France hold him to be their master." In the preface to his *Preces ecclesiasticae*, du Caurroy claims to have "imitated the ancients," the contrapuntal techniques of Josquin, Willaert and Zarlino, whose work he studied. *New Grove Dictionary*, s.v." Du Caurroy," by Paul-André Gaillard, p. 669.

[222] This phrase is omitted in the 1724 edition.

[223] As Delair suggests, augmented and diminished chords were rarely used by French composers, but were mostly associated with Italian repertoire. In the eighteenth century, as French composers came under increasing Italian influence, they began to experiment with dissonance in their dramatic pieces.

The fourth alone on a note is accompanied by the second and the sixth (A,B).

The fourth followed by a third on the same note is accompanied by the fifth and the octave (A,B).

One can also play the sixth with a fourth which is followed by a third when it occurs on the first note of a cadence, provided that the note on which the fourth is played has the value of at least a half note.

The tritone or augmented fourth is accompanied by the major second and the major sixth on the middle note of a bass which descends three notes in succession.

[26]

The tritone is also accompanied by the second and the sixth when it occurs on a syncopated note (A), or when it follows a natural chord over the same bass note, provided it does not have the value of one beat (*un temps*)[224] but takes the place of a dot,[225] sharing the beat with a note which subsequently descends a degree.

---

[224]A beat (*un temps*) is equivalent to the value of a half note in common time.
[225]Delair means that the 6/4#/2 is played above a quarter note.

The tritone is also sometimes accompanied by the minor third and the sixth when it is played on a note on which one previously played a minor third, as long as this note is not syncopated (A). If it were, it would be necessary to play the second instead of the minor third (B).

The tritone is also sometimes accompanied by the major third [and sixth], when the bass descends afterwards by a semitone to a note on which the natural major chord is played.

In all other instances, the tritone is accompanied by the sixth and the octave (A,B,C,D,E).

Frequently, the tritone is notated like the natural fourth followed by a major third. To distinguish between them, one will observe that the fourth and a sharp signify the natural fourth followed by the major third [in the following cases]: when the bass ascends afterwards a degree (A) or a fourth (B), when the bass descends a minor third to a sharped note (C) or to a note which takes the place of a sharped note, like *Mi* or *Si* (D), or when the bass descends a major third (E).

Ex. 91

In all other cases, the fourth followed by a sharp signifies the tritone.

The tritone is also frequently notated like the natural fourth, by a four alone, but only on notes which do not have the perfect fourth naturally like *Fa* (A), on all flatted notes whose fourths are naturally augmented (B), and on natural notes whose fourth is sharped at the beginning of the clef (C,D).

[27]

Ex. 92

Because the major third never follows the tritone on the same bass note, it is more appropriate to put the sharp after, rather than before, the four. In this way, the major third, which often precedes the tritone, cannot be confused with the tritone or with the natural fourth.

Ex. 93

It would be desirable if the augmented fourth had a particular sign which would distinguish it from the natural fourth followed by a major third; this, however, would necessitate correcting all the opera scores in which there is no such differentiation.[226]

The fifth by itself indicates the natural chord.

The false fifth, or diminished fifth, is accompanied by the minor third and the minor sixth, when the bass ascends a semitone.

Ex. 94a

---

[226]As Delair explained at the beginning of this chapter, the sharps and flats are placed after the figures they alter in French operas. The ambiguity of this and other figured-bass notational idiosyncrasies, such as the inconsistent use of the slash, irritated Rameau as well. (See his *Dissertation*, p. 4).

This rule holds unless one is obliged to play an augmented fifth on the second note of the ascending semitone. In this case, the octave is played on the first bass note, and the seventh is sounded as a passing tone to the augmented fifth on the second note. Alternatively, the seventh may by played simultaneously with the augmented fifth on the second note.[227]

The diminished fifth is accompanied by the third and the octave when the bass ascends a fourth (A), or descends a minor third (B).

The diminished fifth is sometimes indicated by a single five, like the natural fifth, but only on notes which have the diminished fifth naturally, such as *Si* (A) and sharped notes (B), or on natural notes whose fifths are flatted at the beginning of the clef (C,D).

The augmented fifth is accompanied by the third and the seventh (A) or by the ninth (B).[228]

---

[227]This paragraph and Example 94b are from the 1724 edition.
[228]In the 1724 edition, Delair adds: "The augmented fifth is accompanied by the third and the seventh if the ninth has not been prepared; if the ninth has been prepared, the augmented fifth is accompanied by the third, the seventh, and the ninth." See Ex. 97b and Ex. 97c.

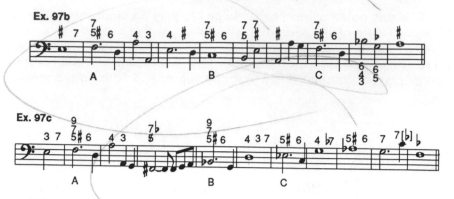

Ex. 97b

Ex. 97c

The sixth alone on a note is accompanied by the third and the octave.

Ex. 98

[28]

It must be noted that, with the minor sixth, one plays the minor third (A); with the major sixth, one can play either the minor third (B) or the major third (C).

Ex. 99

The sixth following the seventh on the same bass note is often accompanied by the fourth.

Ex. 100

One always plays a fourth with a minor sixth which follows a seventh, as long as the third that is played with the seventh is major.

Ex. 101

The major sixth is accompanied by the minor third and the fourth when, afterwards, the bass descends a tone to a note on which the natural chord is played (A,B), provided that the note which makes the fourth has been sounded above the preceding [bass] note. If not, it should not be played (C).

Ex. 102

The major sixth is also thus accompanied when the bass ascends three notes in succession, and when it is played on the middle [bass] note.[229]

Ex. 103

The seventh by itself on a note is accompanied by the third and the fifth.

Ex. 104

The seventh is also accompanied by the second, the fourth and the fifth,[230] if desired, provided that it is preceded and followed by a natural chord. This seventh, as well as the second which accompanies it, should always be major.

Ex. 105

---

[229]In the 1724 edition, Delair specifies that the "middle note of the bass" refers to the "second degree of the key."

[230]In the 1724 edition, Delair adds that the seventh is accompanied by the second, the fourth, and the fifth in major keys, and the [second, fourth, and] sixth in minor keys.

The seventh followed by the sixth is accompanied by the third and the fifth, or by the octave,[231] if the note on which the seventh is played is slow-moving (A,B). If it is a fast note, the third and the octave, but not the fifth, are played, or the third is doubled instead of the octave (C).[232]

Ex. 106a

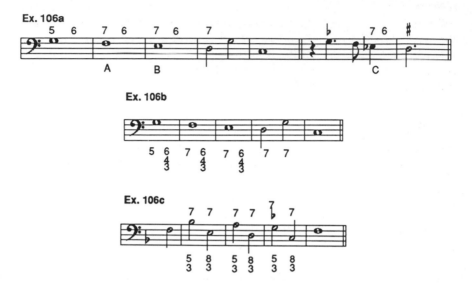

Ex. 106b

Ex. 106c

The diminished seventh is accompanied by the third and the diminished fifth.

Ex. 107

The octave indicates the natural chord.

[29]

The ninth or the second, which is played on the beginning of a note, is accompanied by the third and the fifth. It can be major (A) or minor (B).

Ex. 108

---

[231]The rest of this phrase is omitted in the 1724 edition. In the example from the *Nouveau traité*, Delair gives 6/4/3 as the chord of resolution. (See Ex. 106b).

[232]In the 1724 edition, Delair, adds: "Seventh chords played above a bass progression that ascends and descends by a fifth are accompanied alternately by the third and the fifth, and the octave and the third." (See Ex. 106c).

Extraordinary Accompaniments

Most of the preceding [figured] intervals can be accompanied in still other ways. These other realizations, not being ordinary, are figured in the manner shown below. Examples include the following: the fourth followed by the third, with which one sometimes plays the sixth (A); the diminished fifth, with which one sometimes plays the diminished seventh instead of the sixth (B); the seventh, with which one sometimes plays the fourth (C); the ninth, with which one sometimes also plays the fourth (D) or the seventh (E).

One would have hoped, perhaps, that I had written out the examples of basso continuo realizations in harpsichord tablature, but I decided that that would be much less useful than if all the chords were reduced to only four different ones, according to the disposition of the notes of which they are composed, as one will see in the following examples. [Before proceeding], notice that there are twenty-three chords, differing as much in their nature as in their accompaniments.[233]

Ex. 110: *Difference Between Figured Intervals and Their Accompaniments*

Accompaniments:									
Figured Intervals:									

Accompaniments: 5 6 6/4♯ 8/5 8/5 8/6 5 6/2 8/6 6 3

Figured Intervals: 4/2 4/2 2♯ 3 4 4 7/4 4♯ 4♯ 4♯ 6/3 5

Accompaniments: 6/3 3 8/3 3 3 8/3 4/3 5/3 8/3 4/2 5/3 3

Figured Intervals: 5 7♭ 5 7 9 66♯7 7 7♯ 9 9/7 [30] 5   5♯ 5♯

---

[233]Recognizing the ambiguity of a figured-bass notation in which only the characteristic interval is notated on the continuo bass, Delair is one of the first theorists to organize figured-bass signatures into a table. He places the figured interval on the lower line and, on the upper, he lists the other intervals which must be added by the accompanist to complete the realization. See Burchill, p. 16.

The following table shows that twelve of the chords relate by the disposition of the right hand to the natural chord.[234] The others, as accompanied ordinarily, relate either to the ninth or to the diminished fifth. Only the fourth accompanied by the fifth bears no relation to the others.

Ex. 111: *Table of Chords Which Share the Same Right-Hand Accompaniment*

Chords Which Relate to the Natural Chord

Chords Which Relate to the Ninth and False Fifth Chords

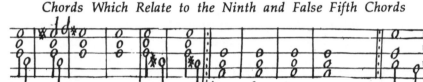

Observing the relations of these chords to one another, one sees that it would be useless to write out all the examples in score. It is enough to give examples of the chords to which the others relate, and to show all the ways in which they can be varied. This can be learned easily when one observes that each chord contains three different intervals without counting the bass, and thus can be varied in three ways. For example, the

---

[234]In order to simplify the task of learning to associate the figures with a particular hand position at the harpsichord or theorbo, Delair reduces most of the chords to three, by grouping together those chords that share the same right-hand realization. In this way, he anticipates Rameau's theory of chord inversion.

natural chord is varied by beginning with the octave (A,B), or with the third (C,D), or with the fifth (E,F). The little notes indicate the ornaments which can be made on each of these chords.

Ex. 112: *Ornamented Realization, Showing the Different Dispositions of the Natural Chord*

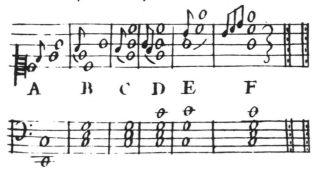

It is the same for the seventh, the diminished fifth and the fourth.

Ex. 113: *The Different Dispositions of the Ninth, False Fifth and Fourth Chords*

[31]

Chords relating to the ones discussed, above, differ only in the bass; accordingly, one can make use of the preceding manners of realization for the chords corresponding to those in the examples.

Putting the examples in score is all the more useless since this would cause one to learn by rote. Instead, by putting simply what is encountered on the continuo basses, one is obliged to think about each rule, and to learn accompaniment by reasoning.

All notes in the preceding accompaniments are not absolutely necessary. It is possible to omit certain ones, principally on instruments such as the theorbo--where the hand labors in many places, and one does not find all the desired accompaniments with ease. In fast tempos, when it is almost impossible to play all the [notes] indicated by the figures, as in the above examples, the third suffices for any chord except for the second and the fourth. To facilitate [accompaniment] on all instruments, notice that in fast tempos, the third is a sufficient accompaniment to the fifth, the sixth, the seventh, the octave, and the ninth, whatever the species of chord:

5   6   7   8   9
3   3   3   3   3

Similarly, when the fourth takes the place of the third, it is a sufficient accompaniment to the intervals to which it is joined. For example, the fourth is sufficient to the fifth, the sixth, the seventh, the octave, and the ninth, when it is figured with these intervals:

5   6   7   8   9
4   4   4   4   4

There are also some chords--those whose notes are a third apart--which do not absolutely require the third. These chords are enough in themselves to make a complete harmony. For example, the second and the fourth, as well as the third and the fifth, are sufficient by themselves. One will see these and other sufficient accompaniments in the following demonstration:

[32]

Sufficient Accompaniments

4 5 6 7 8 9
2 3 4 5 6 7

Nevertheless, when possible, it is better to play all the notes suitable to the accompaniment of each [figured] interval, especially on the harpsichord, the instrument on which one can play them all most easily.

V

Rules for the Addition of Figures Omitted on Basses, which also Serve as Rules for Accompanying Unfigured Basses

Inasmuch as music consists only of intervals, either ascending or descending, we will point out everything that must be done on each interval of the bass, beginning with the ascending intervals, and concluding with the descending intervals.[235]

It must first be remarked that all descending intervals relate to ascending ones, although they are named differently; thus, what we will say about ascending intervals applies to the descending intervals to which they relate. To understand this clearly, note that the interval of an ascending whole step relates to that of a descending seventh, the interval of an ascending third to that of a descending sixth, that of an ascending fourth to that of a descending fifth, that of an ascending fifth

Ex. 114: *Relationship Between the Ascending and Descending Intervals*

---

[235]Like other seventeenth-century theorists such as Fleury and Bartolotti in France, and Penna and Gasparini in Italy, Delair gives standard realizations for typical bass progressions.

to that of a descending fourth, that of an ascending sixth to that of a descending third, that of an ascending seventh to that of a descending whole step--with this difference, that the intervals which are major in ascending are minor in descending, and those which are minor in ascending are major in descending.

The sixth is played on sharped notes (A), on *Mi* (B) and on *Si* (C), unless the following bass note ascends a fourth, or descends a major semitone or a minor third. In these cases, the natural chord must be played (D,E,F).

Ex. 115

Ordinarily, when the sixth is played on a sharped note, the octave [above the bass] is not doubled.

It should be noted that when there are several sharps after the clef, these sharped notes take the place of *Mi* and *Si*, and when there are several flats, the notes just below these flats take the place of *Mi* and *Si*; the chords appropriate to *Mi* and *Si* are to be played on these notes.

Rules for the Ascending Intervals

Rules for the Interval of an Ascending Semitone or a Descending Major Seventh

When the bass ascends a semitone to a note that does not take the sixth, the minor third and minor sixth are played on the first bass note. The diminished fifth is passed on the last part of this note (A). The sixth and fifth are played together when the diminished fifth has been sounded above the preceding [bass note] (B), or if the tempo is fast (C).

Ex. 116

When the bass ascends a semitone to a note that takes a sixth, the major sixth must be played on the first note (A), provided that the second note does not lead to a cadence. If so, the minor sixth must be played on the first note (B).

Ex. 117

The sixth should not be omitted on the first [bass] note of this interval, even if the second note does not take a sixth (A,B).

Ex. 118

Rules for the Interval of an Ascending Tone or a Descending Minor Seventh

When the bass ascends a tone, if the seventh or sixth is not marked on the second note, the seventh can be passed on the end of the first note.

Ex. 119

[34]

If the bass ascends a tone to arrive at an immediate cadence, the third above the first note should be of the same species as the natural third of the final. Thus, if the final has a minor third naturally, the third [in the chord] above the first note should also be minor (A), and if the final has a major third, the third above the first note should be major (B).

Ex. 120

If the bass ascends a tone to arrive at an immediate cadence, and if the seventh above the first note has not been sounded above the preceding note, then the sixth and the fifth are played. They may be played either in succession (A) or, if the fifth has been prepared and the tempo is fast, they may be played together (B).

Ex. 121

However, if the seventh has been sounded above the preceding [bass] note, it is ordinarily played. This occurs when the [preceding] note is a fifth (A), a third (B), a degree higher (C), or even a degree lower (D), [than the bass which takes the seventh]. This seventh should be of the same species as the third, such that if the third of the seventh chord is minor, the seventh should also be minor, and if the third is major, the seventh should also be major.

Ex. 122

When the bass ascends a tone to a note that takes a sixth chord, the sixth and fifth are played instead of the seventh, even if the seventh has been sounded above the preceding [bass note].

Ex. 123

When the bass ascends a tone to a note that takes a major third, and a seventh is not played on the first note, then the sixth must be played (A). The fifth, if it has been sounded in the preceding chord, may be played with it (B).

Ex. 124

[35]

One may play a seventh [instead of a sixth] with the fifth on the first note, provided that the bass note which precedes this [two-note progression] is a minor third higher, and one has played a tritone above it. The seventh is played with the fifth if the bass note is [less than] a beat in length (A), but if it is equal to a beat, then the seventh is played only in passing on the last part of the note (B).

Ex. 125

A minor third is always played on the first note of an interval that ascends by a tone when the last note concludes a cadence.

Ex. 126

Rules for the Interval of an Ascending Third or a Descending Sixth

When the bass ascends a minor third, a minor third must be played on the first note (A). If a sixth is played with it, this sixth should also be minor (B).

Ex. 127

When the bass ascends a major third, a major third must be played on the first note (A) and, if the sixth is played with it, the sixth should also be major (B). If a sixth is played on the last note, this sixth should be minor (C).

Ex. 128

When the bass ascends three equal notes, falls back to the first, and then ascends a fifth or fourth, a sixth is played on the third note (A,B,C).

Ex. 129

When the bass ascends the interval of a minor third by conjunct degree, and when the last two notes are only a semitone apart, one observes on these last two notes what has been prescribed above for the interval of an ascending semitone.

Ex. 130

Rules for the Interval of an Ascending Fourth or a Descending Fifth

[36]

When the bass ascends a fourth, a major third should be played on the first note, with a minor seventh as a passing tone (A). This rule holds as long as the preceding bass note is not a minor third higher. If so, it would be necessary to play the minor third on the first note [of the ascending fourth] (B), in progressions that are not cadential. If cadential, then the major third is played (C). If the second note requires a seventh, then the natural third must be played on the first note (D,E). If, after having ascended a fourth, the bass descends a fifth, a minor third must be played on the first note, and a seventh must be played on the following note, even if not marked. This frequently occurs before cadences (F).

Ex. 131

A   B   C   D   E   F

When a minor third is played on the first note of an ascending fourth, a seventh may be played on the second note, provided that the bass ascends afterwards a degree (A) or a fourth (B).

Ex. 132

A   B

Rules for the Interval of an Ascending Fifth or a Descending Fourth

When the bass ascends a fifth, and a fourth is not marked on the second note, the sixth is ordinarily passed on the end of the first note (A). It must be noted that when the third above the second note is major, the passing tone of a sixth should also be major (B), and when the third is minor, the natural sixth is played (C,D).

Ex. 133

A sixth is played on the first note [of the ascending fifth] if the bass has previously descended a third.

[37]

Ex. 134

When the bass ascends a fifth and there is a fourth marked on the second note, a passing tone must not be played on the end of the first.

Ex. 135

When the bass ascends a fifth, if a minor third is played on the second note, then a minor third should also be played on the first (A,B). When a sixth is played on the second note, it should be of the same species as the preceding third, such that if the third of the first note is major, the sixth of the second should also be major (C), and if the third of the first is minor, the sixth of the second should be minor also (D).

Ex. 136

When the bass ascends five notes in succession, and the first four are of equal value--either quarters or eighths--a sixth is played on the third (A,B). This is also done when these notes are dotted, two by two (C,D).

Ex. 137

Rules for the Interval of an Ascending Minor Sixth or a Descending Major Third

When the bass ascends a minor sixth, a minor third must be played on the first note (A), and a major third on the second (C). If a sixth is played with the minor third, it must also be minor (B).

Ex. 138

We will see, below, what must be done with the intervals of an ascending major sixth and a descending minor third, as well as the intervals of an ascending seventh and a descending second. Since these intervals are hardly used at all in ascending, it is more suitable to discuss the descending intervals to which these ascending intervals relate.

Rules for the Descending Intervals

When the bass descends a minor semitone, that is, from a natural note to a note that is flatted or sharped on the same natural note, and a sixth is played on the first bass note, then it is also played on the following note.

[38]

Ex. 139

Rules for the Interval of a Descending Semitone or an Ascending Major Seventh

When the bass descends a semitone to a note that is not sharped, [these rules must be followed]:

If a seventh is not played on the second bass note, then a tritone may be introduced as a passing tone on the end of the first note; a sixth is played on the second (A,B).

If a seventh is played on the second bass note, the natural fourth must be played with the sixth on the end of the first note (C).

However, if a fourth is played on the second bass note, only a major sixth is played on the end of the first note (D).

Ex. 140

One must take care, moreover, that the [above] progression does not terminate in a cadence, and that the first note is not syncopated. Should the two notes terminate in a cadence, the seventh [followed by] the major sixth must be played on the first note, and the natural major chord on the last note.

Ex. 141

One can recognize a cadence by the major third, which should be marked on the second note of the progression, or, if the bass is not figured, one can listen for the termination of the melodic line.

If the first note is a syncopation--that is to say, if it partakes of two beats or of two measures, and begins on the end of one beat or measure and finishes on the beginning of the following beat or measure--then the second and its accompanying chord tones [6/4#/2] are played on the second part of this syncopation, and a sixth and a fifth on the following note (A,B). [The diminished fifth is played with the sixth on the second bass note] as long as the bass ascends a semitone afterwards. If it does not, the diminished fifth is omitted, and only the sixth is played (C).

[39]

Ex. 142

The syncopation may also occur in a three-beat measure, beginning on the first beat and finishing on the second (A,B).

Ex. 143

Rules for the Interval of a Descending Tone or an Ascending Minor Seventh

When the bass descends a tone, if a sixth is not played initially on the first note, then it is ordinarily introduced as a passing tone on the last part of this note. The sixth should always be major (A,B) unless a seventh is played on the second note; in this case, the sixth should be natural (C,D).

Ex. 144

When a major sixth is played on the first note of the interval [of a descending tone], and a natural chord is played on the second note, the third of the sixth chord should be minor.

Ex. 145

When a major sixth has been played on the first note, one should also play a chord above the second note. This is done even if it is only an eighth (A), or a sixteenth note (B), since the major sixth [leading tone] is played above the first note only in order to reach the octave above the second, which must always follow it.

Ex. 146

When the bass descends several notes in succession, a major sixth is played only on the penultimate.

Ex. 147

When a minor sixth is played above the first note of the interval [of a descending tone], and if a sixth is not played on the second, then a seventh is ordinarily played on the second note--provided the bass ascends afterwards a degree (A), or a fourth (B), or if a sixth is played on the second part of the second note (C).

Ex. 148

[40]

If *Sol* precedes (A) or follows *Fa* (B), a minor chord must always be played on *Sol*, unless the bass cadences on *Ut* (C) or on *Mi* (E), or the bass subsequently reaches a cadence on *La* (E), or a tritone is played on *Fa* (F). [In these cases], a major third must be played on *Sol*, even it is preceded or followed by *Fa*.

Ex. 149

This same rule is observed on notes that are a degree above flatted notes. On these notes, one is obliged to play a minor third when they immediately precede (A) or follow flatted notes (B), [with the same exceptions as above], as long as they do not lead to a cadence which descends by a fifth (C) or by a degree (D), and, provided that a tritone is not played on the flatted notes (F). If so, it would be necessary to play a major third on the notes that precede or follow the flatted notes.

Ex. 150

Rules for the Interval of a Descending Minor Third or an Ascending Major Sixth[236]

When the bass descends a minor third, a minor third must always be played on the last note of this interval (A), and a major third on the first (B), unless a diminished fifth is played on the last note. Then, a minor third must be played above the first bass note (C). Take care that the second note does not lead to a cadence--either ascending by fourth or descending by fifth--inasmuch as it would then be necessary to play a major third on the last note of this interval (D).

[41]

Ex. 151

---

[236]Under this heading, Delair also discusses rules for the interval of a descending major third. At the end of the section, he appends two remarks concerning the interval of a descending diminished fourth and a descending diminished fifth.

If a sixth were played on the first note, it would have to be major.

Ex. 152

Even if the first note of the interval [of a descending minor third] is only the second note of a beat, one should not neglect to play a minor third on the last note.

Ex. 153

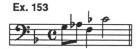

When the bass descends a major third, a major third is played on the last note (A). A minor third is played on the first note (B), unless the bass cadences on a note a fifth lower. Then, it would be necessary to play a major third on the first note (C,D).

Ex. 154

If a sixth is played on the first note, it should be minor.

Ex. 155

When the bass descends a major third to a flatted note, or to *Ut* or *Fa*, and when a major third is played on the first, a sixth is always played on the last note, as can be seen in the preceding example [Ex. 154] (C,D).

When the bass descends three notes in succession, outlining the interval of a minor third, a minor third is played on the last note (A), unless this note terminates in or leads to a cadence, in which case, a major third must be played (B,C).

Ex. 156

When the bass descends three notes in succession, the last two by a tone, the species of the sixth on the first note should be suitable to the interval of the third [outlined by the bass]. A major sixth with a minor third is played on the second note, and a natural chord is played on the last (A,B).

Ex. 157

A   B

[42]

If a seventh is played on the last of these notes, a natural sixth must be played on the second note. One is not obliged to play a sixth on the first.

Ex. 158

When the bass descends a [minor] third by conjunct degree, and a major third is played on the first note, a tritone is ordinarily played on the second, and a sixth is played on the last (A). If the third of the first note is naturally major, this rule holds only if the last two notes descend by a semitone (B,C). If the last two notes descend by a tone, one must use the rule which prescribes that a sixth be played on the first two notes, and a natural chord on the third (D,E). One should make use of this same rule if the last two notes terminate in a cadence, even though they may be only a semitone apart (F).

Ex. 159

A   B   C   D   E   F

When the bass descends three notes in succession to a sharped note, if a major third is not played on the first, a major sixth must be played instead, with a natural chord on the second note, and a sixth above the last.

Ex. 160

One must take care that the first of these notes does not terminate a cadence, because, if it does, a natural chord would be played on the first, a tritone on the second, and a sixth on the last, conforming to one of the preceding rules (A,B,C).

Ex. 161

A   B   C

[43]

When the bass descends four or five notes in succession, the preceding rules affect only the last three notes, with this difference: If the last of the four bass notes is not sharped and if the first two descend by a tone, the second note takes the natural or augmented fourth, as encountered naturally, with the second and the sixth (A). Ordinarily, a major sixth is played on the third note, unless the last two notes descend by a semitone (the last note still not being sharped). Then, an augmented fourth and a sixth must be played on the third note, and a sixth on the last note (B).

Ex. 162

A   B

Concerning the preceding example, be advised that one is not obliged to play a minor third on the first of the four notes. If a minor third is played, it would be necessary to play a third instead of a fourth with the sixth on the second note.

Ex. 163

When the bass descends five notes in succession, and the last two notes descend by a tone, a major third is played on the first note, a tritone on the second, and a sixth on the third and fourth, in accordance with the preceding rules.

Ex. 164

When the bass descends several notes in succession to a sharped note, one does not do anything extraordinary; one simply plays a major sixth on the first of the last three notes, a natural chord on the second, and a sixth on the last, conforming to the rule discussed above, which deals with the interval of a minor third.

Ex. 165

The preceding rules are also observed on eighth notes, and even on sixteenths.

Ex. 166

When the bass descends a diminished fourth, a sixth is played on the first note.

Ex. 167

When the bass descends a diminished fifth, a minor third is played on the first note.

Ex. 168

General Rules Applicable Equally to All the Intervals of Unfigured Basses

[44]

Two successive fifths or octaves in parallel motion are prohibited. If someone were to ask me why parallel fifths and octaves are not allowed, while consecutive thirds and sixths are permitted, I would reply that the beauty of music consists in modulation and in variety, and there can be no beauty in the repetition of successive octaves and fifths, since both these intervals have a fixed range, fixed not only by the number of degrees, but also by the number of tones and semitones they contain. This is why the repetition of these intervals is forbidden. The third and the sixth, on the other hand, not being fixed in the number of semitones they contain, being sometimes major and sometimes minor, provide variety and, as a consequence, are permitted. For this same reason, composers of the past prohibited two successive thirds of the same species. The only reason that two successive fifths or octaves are not allowed is owing to this defect of variety or modulation. The reader will be convinced of this if he observes that two fifths in contrary motion are permitted, as well as two fifths of different species--that is to say, one perfect, and one false-- because in this way, there is modulation and variety.

At the beginning of a piece, one ordinarily plays a major third on the first note one finds that is a fifth higher than the final or the principal of the piece being accompanied. Thus, supposing that the final is *Sol*, one will play a major chord on the first *Re* one finds (A), and if the final is *La*, one will play a major chord on the first *Mi* one finds (B), with this exception: If the note a fifth above the final descends afterwards a minor third to a note on which a diminished fifth is played, then a minor third, rather than a major third, must be played (C).

Ex. 169

A fourth is not played on the first note of a cadence if it has not been sounded above the preceding [bass] note, [as] is encountered when the bass ascends a fourth (A) or descends a third (B). In all other instances, the fourth is ordinarily played, as long as the tempo is not too fast (C,D,E).

[45]

Ex. 170

One is obliged to play the passing tone of a seventh or diminished fifth [in certain bass progressions]. When the notes which make up these chords have been sounded above the preceding [bass] note, one holds them the entire length of the note, instead of playing them as passing tones only on the end of it.

Ex. 171

Ordinarily, one plays a major third on a note which is a fifth higher than the final of the following cadence (A,B,C).

Ex. 172

The ninth and the seventh should be of the same species as the consonances that precede them, such that, if the third or the sixth that precedes them is flatted, these dissonances should also be flatted; if they have been sharped, the seventh and the ninth should also be sharped (A,B,C,D,E).

Ex. 173

When the bass ascends a degree (A), a fourth (B), or descends a third (C), and when a sixth is figured on the last part of the second note of these intervals, a seventh can be played on the first part of the note, even if it is not notated.

Ex. 174

A dissonance must be resolved on the [bass] note that follows it, even if the note of resolution is on the second part of a beat, and whether or not the bass moves in conjunct motion (A,B,C,D).

[46]

Ex. 175

When several bass notes descend successively to a cadence, a seventh is ordinarily played on the first part of these notes, and a sixth on the second part.

Ex. 176

The same rule applies even if there are eighth notes between these descending notes, if the eighth notes are only for the ornamentation of the line.

Ex. 177

A seventh is ordinarily played on a note that ascends by conjunct degree to the final cadence. This is done even if the note which makes the seventh has not been sounded in the previous chord (A), or when a seventh has been played on the preceding bass note (B).

Ex. 178

A slur over two notes indicates that the chord played on the first is to be sustained over the second.

Ex. 179

[To determine what chords to play above unfigured basses], one should defer to the [bass] intervals that precede, and give preference to their requirements, rather than to those that follow.[237] For example, if the bass descends a minor third, and ascends afterward by fourth, a minor third must be played on the middle note, without regard for the interval of a fourth that follows--which would require that a major third be played instead of a minor.

---

[237]In giving preference to the bass interval which precedes rather than follows a note, to determine what chord to play, Delair differs from Fleury, who recommends looking at the bass interval which follows. See Burchill, p. 17.

Ex. 180

It is the same for all notes that are found between two intervals, each of which requires a different chord. One must give preference to the preceding over the following interval, and must play the chords that conform to the rules for the preceding intervals preferentially over those suitable to the interval that follows.

Very few chords are played in fast pieces and in slow recitatives, where chords are separated by some silence in order to feature the voice.

[47]

After having acquired a knowledge of the chords, one must learn the value of the notes, not only to give each note the appropriate duration, but also to distinguish those on which one should play a chord from those on which one should do nothing at all. It will be seen that chords are not played on all the notes.

The value of notes cannot be absolutely fixed, because we use different meters which increase or diminish their value. Thus, it is necessary to begin by knowing the different meters, so that, afterwards, the different values of the notes can be distinguished accordingly.

VI

Rules for Knowing the Meters and the Values of Notes According to the Differences in these Meters

There are two kinds of meter (*mesure*), that is to say, ordinary and extraordinary.[238]

There are three types of simple meter, that is to say, two-beat, three-beat, and four-beat meter, each of which has its own different [time] signature.[239]

The meter of two beats is indicated by a two or by a slashed C (¢). The meter of three beats is indicated by a three alone, or a three and a two, or by a three preceded by a C; and the meter of four beats is indicated by a C alone.[240]

---

[238]Simple and compound meter.

[239]Delair is one of the first to make a tentative attempt to categorize the various meter signs according to the number of beats in the measure. He classifies signature "2" as duple; "3," "C3" and "3/2" as triple, and "C" as quadruple meter. This method of classification became standard practice in the eighteenth century. See Houle, pp. 36-38.

[240]The reader should keep in mind that, in the baroque period, meter was associated with tempo. The theorists Masson, Jacques Hotteterre and Saint Lambert have documented the association of meter signs with various tempi. (See Harris-Warrick, pp. xiv-xvii.) Hotteterre gives a thorough description of various meters and their corresponding tempi: "Quadruple meter is indicated by a C. It is composed of four quarter notes, or the equivalent, and is usually beaten very slowly. The meter [of barred C] is indicated by a ¢. Like the preceding one it is composed of four quarter notes. Its usual movement is four quick beats or two slow beats. The [two-beat] meter is usually lively [*vive*] and detached [*piqué*]. ("*Cette Mesure se marque par un C. Elle est composée de 4 noires ou de l'équivalent. Elle se bat a 4 temps et pour l'ordinaire tres lentement. Cette Mesure [du C. barré] se marque par ce signe, ¢. Elle est composée ainsi que la precedente de 4 noires. Son mouvement ordinaire est 4 temps legers ou 2 temps lents. Cette Mesure [a 2 temps] se marque par un 2 simple. Elle est ordinairement vive et piquée*"), Jacques Hotteterre, *l'Art de préluder sur la flûte traversière* (Paris: l'auteur, 1719), pp. 57-58. Delair hints at metrical/temporal relationships by

Ex. 181: *Relationship of Time Signatures to Tempo*

Note values are fixed by two or four-beat meter, not by three-beat meter, since simple triple meter relates, in terms of note value, to four-beat meter, and double triple meter relates to two-beat meter, as we will see hereafter.

[48]

Names and Values of Notes

There are five different note values: whole notes, half notes, quarters, eighths, and sixteenths.

Ex. 182: *Quantity of Notes Necessary for Measures of Two and Four Beats*

Sixteen Sixteenths
Eight Eighths
Four Quarters
Two Halves
One Whole

I will not discuss maximas, no longer used since we began using barlines. They were written in this way, and had the following values:

Ex. 183: *Maximas*

---

writing descriptive adjectives under his illustration of time signatures, corroborating several of Hotteterre's observations. Concerning duple meter, Delair describes the beats in the meter "2" as fast (*legères*), and those in "C slash" as slow (*lents*). He makes the same distinction for triple meter signatures. The meter "3" is labeled fast (*leger*), and that of C3, slow (*lent*).

A dot after a note augments the value of the note by one half.

Ex. 184: *Dotted Notes*

| Measure and a half | Three quarters of a measure | A quarter and a half | Three quarters of a quarter |

Measures of two and four beats do not differ in the quantity of notes they contain as follows:

Quantity of Notes Necessary for Measures of Two and Four Beats
Ex. 185

Measure of two beats:

Measure of four beats:

The simple triple meter relates to the meter of four beats in that one plays a quarter note or the equivalent for each beat in both kinds of meter. The double triple meter relates to the meter of two beats in that one plays a half note or the equivalent for each beat.[241] These meters differ only in that the triple meters have one beat more or less than the meters of two or four beats.

[49]

Triple Meters

Ex. 186

Simple triple:

Double triple:

---

[241]The double triple, or 3/2 meter, was an old-fashioned time signature which had its origins in the proportional notation of the Renaissance. According to J.-J. Rousseau, by the mid-eighteenth century "this meter was no longer used except in France, where even it was beginning to be abolished." ("Cette mesure n'est plus en usage qu'en France, où même elle commence à s'abolir.") Rousseau, *Dictionnaire*, s.v. "Double-triple," p. 178.

It would be useful to have a knowledge of the rests. Although rare in continuo basses, they are nevertheless encountered occasionally-- especially in symphonies, overtures, or other fugal pieces. Note that there are seven kinds of rests:

Ex. 187: *Names and Values of Rests*

Extraordinary meters are indicated by two different numbers, one above the other. The number below indicates the quality of the notes of which the measure is composed in relation to meters of two and four beats. Thus, if the lower figure is a one, the measure should be composed of whole notes; if it is a two, the measure should be composed of half notes; if it is a four, it should be composed of eighths, and if it is a sixteen, the measure would be composed of sixteenths.

The upper figure indicates the quantity. For example, a four above an eight indicates four eighths, a six above a four indicates six quarters, etc., as we will see in the following example, which shows all possible meters. Figures marked on top in extraordinary meters indicate the type of notes. Figures marked on the bottom indicate the quality of the notes.

Ex. 188: *Extraordinary Meters*

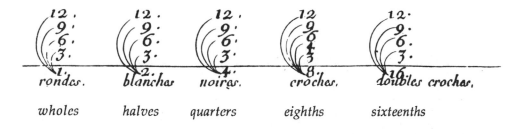

| wholes | halves | quarters | eighths | sixteenths |

Rules for Knowing on Which Notes to Play Chords

[50]

A chord is played only on the first note of each downbeat (*frapé*)[242] and each upbeat (*levé*) in ordinary meters of two, three and four beats, as well as in extraordinary meters in which the three predominates, when the bass proceeds by conjunct degree, either ascending or descending. This rule holds unless one of the preceding rules requires that a chord be played on the second part of the downbeat or upbeat.

In extraordinary meters in which the six predominates and one plays three eighth notes or three quarter notes during each downbeat and each upbeat, a chord is played on the first and last note of each beat. In meters in which the nine or twelve predominates (which would be either in a three- or a four-beat meter, with three quarters or three eighth notes for each beat) a chord is played only on the first note of each beat; the [other] two notes [of the beat] are passed over without playing a chord.[243]

On the harpsichord, a chord should be played on all notes which proceed by disjunct degree, no matter what the meter, even if the notes only have the value of half a beat. However, on the theorbo, since this is impossible in pieces in which the tempo is fast, it suffices to play a chord on the first of each downbeat and the first of each upbeat.

Repeating chords which have been sounded above preceding [bass] notes is an encumbrance which should be avoided. In pieces in a fast tempo, one may be satisfied with playing, on [bass] notes in the second part of the beat, only the notes that have not been sounded in the preceding chord, holding over those notes from the preceding chord which are appropriate to the following one. For example, when the bass ascends a third, and a sixth chord is played on the second note, one can dispense with playing any chord on the second note, since all the chord tones above the first bass note are also suitable to the second. It is useless to repeat them, especially when the tempo is fast.

[51]

---

[242]Saint Lambert tells us that in seventeenth- and eighteenth-century France, the orchestra leader kept time by beating his hand or a rolled paper on a table (See Harris-Warrick, p. 39). Apparently, the sound of the stick was so loud, that it caused Rousseau to complain : "To what degree are the ears not shocked at the Paris *Opéra* from the disagreeable and continuous noise made by he who beats the *Mesure*, with his stick. . . ." ("*Combien les oreilles ne sont-elles pas choquées à l'Opéra de Paris du bruit désagréable & continuel que fait, avec son bâton, celui qui bat la Mesure. . . .*") Rousseau, *Dictionnaire*, s.v. "*Battre la Mesure*," p. 52.

[243]Delair classifies the compound signatures 6/4 and 6/8 as compound duple, 9/4 and 9/8 as compound triple, and 12/4 and 12/8 as compound quadruple meters, respectively.

Ex. 189

When the bass descends a third (A) or ascends a sixth (B), and if a seventh is played on the second note, one can hold the chord tones played on the first note through the second note; only the bass note is played. The same rule applies when a sixth is played on the first note (C).

Ex. 190

When the bass descends a third and then ascends a fourth, one does not play any chord at all on the second note.

Ex. 191

When the bass descends a fifth and then ascends a degree, one plays only the third of the chord on the middle note, holding down the chord tones from the first chord.

Ex. 192

The same rule is observed in all fast tempos; one holds, on the second note of each beat, appropriate chord tones from the preceding chord.

When the bass ascends three equal notes in tempos which are somewhat slow, it is good to play the third on the second [bass] note in order to maintain the harmony, even though this note does not absolutely require a chord.

Ex. 193

When the bass ascends a degree (A) or a fourth (B), or descends a third (C) or a degree (D) from a note on which a sixth is played, and provided that the bass subsequently ascends a degree or a fourth, a seventh can be played on the middle note, and a natural chord on the last note.

[52]

Ex. 194

A   B   C

When the bass ascends or descends several notes in succession, and the notes are only worth a half or a quarter of a beat, a chord is played only on the first of each beat.

Ex. 195

VII

Rule for Knowing [the Key] of a Piece

To ascertain the [key] of a composition,[244] one looks at the final of the bass. If the bass ends in *Ut*, the piece is said to be in *C Sol Ut*; if it finishes in *Re*, then it is in *D La Re*, and so forth with the other keys.

To know if the composition is major or minor, one observes the third of the last note. If it is minor throughout, naturally or artificially, the piece is minor. If the third of the final is major through the course of the piece, naturally or artificially, the piece is major. For example, if a piece is in *G Re Sol*, one looks to see whether *Si*, which is the third, is flatted at the beginning of the clef, since if it is, the piece will be in *G Re Sol* minor. If it is not, the piece will be in *G Re Sol* major. It is the same for the other keys.

Rules for Transpositions

[53]

A piece is called transposed in terms of composition and accompaniment if, during the course of the piece, the final does not have the third which suits it naturally, the third being outside its natural state by some sharp or flat which augments it or diminishes it by a

---

[244]In the transition from the church modes to the major/minor system, the concepts of tone, mode, and key were not uniformly defined. Delair's avoidance of the terms key and mode in this passage points to the confusion surrounding their usage. For Masson and Loulié, tone and mode were synonymous. Saint Lambert has been recognized as being the first to make a clear distinction between tone, the tonic note and mode, the intervallic species. Delair makes the same distinction here, but eschews using the words key and mode. Rameau codifies the terminology, writing that the tone, meaning the key of a piece, is determined by its tonic note and its mode (major or minor).

semitone more or less than it has naturally.[245] Thus, there is no transposed piece without a sharp or flat, although there could be a flat or a sharp at the beginning of the clef in some of the natural modes, as we will see by the following discussion.

Aside from the sharps or flats that are placed at the beginning of the clef to change the nature of the thirds in transposed modes, others are frequently encountered. These re-establish the natural order of the notes in a piece; transposed pieces in major relate to *Ut*, and transposed pieces in minor relate to *Re*, since all the transposed modes relate to these modes.[246] In accompaniment, these sharps or flats prevent false intervals and provide cadences for the essential pitches of each mode. It is first necessary to know the essential pitches of the modes. We will see afterwards what cadences are, in relation to accompaniment. This knowledge will direct us to which of the notes should be sharped or flatted in the different modes.

Rules for Knowing the Essential Pitches of Each Mode

Each mode has three essential pitches, each of which is a third higher than the other.[247] The three essential pitches of *Ut* are *Ut, Mi, Sol*; the three essential pitches of *Re* are *Re, Fa, La*, etc.

The first pitch is called the principal; it serves as fundamental and gives the name to the piece. It is also called the final, because one always concludes with this pitch. The second is called the mediant, falling between the other two essential pitches; the third is called the dominant, the highest of the three pitches.

---

[245]With the increasing numbers of different keys being used as the eighteenth century approached, theorists such as Delair attempted to devise theories of modal transposition to categorize the new keys. Going beyond the familiar definition he gave In Chapter I, "Rules for Knowing the Clefs, and the Notes on the Harpsichord," here Delair sets forth the concept of transposition as a means of classifying keys. He states that it is the position of the third above the final which determines whether or not a mode is transposed. If it falls on a natural, the mode is natural; if it falls on an accidental, the mode is transposed.

[246]Delair uses the scales of *Ut* and *Re* as prototypes for the major and minor scales. For major keys and minor sharp keys, he uses modern key signatures, and, for minor flat keys, he follows the Dorian system (based on *Re*), in which the keys have one sharp more or one flat less than today's signatures.

[247]Delair reiterates here the modal theories set forth by Zarlino, whereby the scale degrees 1, 3, and 5 serve as primary pitches for both melodic and harmonic construction. In the 1724 edition, Delair lists the seventh, or leading tone, as an essential pitch as well, in accordance with emerging tonal theory in the eighteenth century. See "General Rules."

Ex. 196: *Essential Pitches of the Mode*

Each pitch has its own cadences.

[54]

Cadence is a certain conclusion of the melody that the ear expects, after a progression that prepares it. It must be remarked that, to make a cadence on a bass note, it is necessary that the fourth below be perfect. Thus, it is necessary that all the essential pitches of every mode, whether minor or major, have a perfect fourth in descending. If they do not have it naturally, then one makes up for this defect by putting a sharp or a flat immediately after the clef. This is the second principle of the flats or sharps which are put at the beginning of the clefs.

It must be noted, in addition, that when ascending or descending by conjunct degree, the distance between notes cannot exceed one natural tone. For example, one may not ascend from a semitone to a sharped note, as from *Fa* natural to *Sol* sharp, or descend from a sharped note to a natural semitone or to a flatted note, as from *Ut* sharp to *Si* flat, or from *Sol* sharp to *Fa* natural. When these intervals are encountered, not only in the bass but also in the accompaniment, one makes up for this deficiency by sharping the semitones, or flatting the tones at the beginning of the clef. This is the third principle of the sharps and flats found at the beginning of a piece. Thus, the sharps and flats at the beginning of the clefs serve three functions: to alter the thirds, to supply the [accidentals] necessary for cadences, and to prevent false intervals.

Having assumed these rules, one must then look in detail at the notes that should be sharped or flatted in each mode, natural or transposed. Without this knowledge, it would be impossible to accompany most Italian pieces, since one frequently finds these in a transposed mode, in which the flats or sharps natural to the mode of the piece are not marked. There is only a flat or a sharp on the first note to warn of the mode of the piece. It is necessary to know which notes should be sharped or flatted in each mode, since without this knowledge, one would play major chords where there should be minor ones in transposed pieces in the minor [mode], and one would play minor chords where there should be major ones in transposed pieces in the major [mode].

Knowing the sharps and flats appropriate to each key is also necessary because, in Italian pieces, frequent changes in mode or key completely disturb the order of the notes and chords.

Rules for Knowing Which Notes Should Be Sharped or Flatted in Each Particular Key, Either Natural or Transposed

C Sol Ut natural or major has neither sharp nor flat, since its third and the cadences of its essential pitches are natural to the key.

Examples of Cadences: *Principal, Mediant, and Dominant*

[55]

Ex. 197

C Sol Ut minor has the flats of *Mi* and *Si* naturally. The first flat changes the nature of the third, and the second furnishes the cadence of *Mi* [flat], the mediant.

Ex. 198

D La Re natural or minor has no flats or sharps, since the third and the cadences of the essential pitches are natural to the key.

Ex. 199

D La Re major has *Fa* and *Ut* sharps. The first sharp changes the nature of the third, and the second furnishes the cadence of *Fa* [sharp], the mediant.

Ex. 200

E Si Mi natural or minor has *Fa* sharp in order to furnish the cadence of *Si*, the dominant.

[56]

Ex. 201

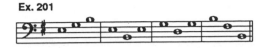

E Si Mi major has the sharps of *Ut, Re, Fa,* and *Sol* naturally. *Sol* sharp changes the nature of the third. *Re* and *Fa* sharps furnish the cadences of *Sol* sharp and *Si,* the mediant and the dominant. *Ut* sharp prevents the false interval between *Ut* natural and *Re* sharp.

Ex. 202

F Ut Fa natural or major has the third and the cadences of the essential pitches naturally. Nevertheless, one does not neglect to flatten *Si,* even though it does not enter into any cadence, to avoid the false interval between *Fa* and *Si.*

Ex. 203

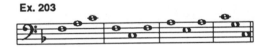

F Ut Fa minor has the flats of *La, Si,* and *Mi* naturally. *La* flat changes the nature of the third, *Si* flat prevents the false interval between *La* flat and *Si* natural, and *Mi* flat furnishes the cadence of *Lu* flat, the mediant.

Ex. 204

G Re Sol natural or major has *Fa* sharp naturally in order to furnish the cadence of *Si,* the mediant.

Ex. 205

G Re Sol minor has *Si* flat naturally, in order to change the nature of the third.

Ex. 206

A *Mi La* natural or minor has the third and the cadences of the essential pitches naturally.

Ex. 207

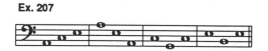

[57]

A *Mi La* major has the sharps of *Ut, Fa,* and *Sol* naturally. The first sharp changes the nature of the third, *Sol* sharp provides the cadence of *Ut,* the mediant, and *Fa* sharp prevents the false interval between *Fa* natural and *Sol* sharp.

Ex. 208

B *Fa Si* flat major has *Mi* flat because it is necessary that the principal pitch of the key have the perfect fifth in descending. *Si* is flatted for the same reason that it is in the key of *F Ut Fa* natural.

Ex. 209

B *Fa Si* minor has the sharps of *Fa* and *Ut.* The first sharp furnishes the cadence of *Si,* the principal pitch, and *Ut* sharp furnishes the cadence of *Fa* sharp, the dominant.

Ex. 210

All the notes which are sharped or flatted at the beginning of the clefs should also be sharped or flatted in the intervals containing [these notes]. For example, if *Mi* is flatted in the bass at the beginning of the clef, all intervals containing *Mi* should be minor. It is the same for the other sharps and the flats at the beginning of the clefs.

VIII

General Rules Concerning the Manner of Accompanying on the Harpsichord

There are several ways of accompanying on the harpsichord. Some people play only the bass with the left hand, doing the accompaniments with the right hand. Others play the chords with the left hand as well as the right. To decide between these two ways, I would say that both of them are good, provided that one uses the first manner of accompanying only for basses which are in a fast tempo, and the second manner for those in a slow tempo.

Most chords played by the left hand serve to fill in any gap which may be encountered between the two hands, since the most essential chord tones should ordinarily be played by the right hand.

When a dissonance is marked on the bass, it should ordinarily be played by the right hand, together with the other essential notes of the chord. The left hand may play the remaining chord tones, or double the notes played by the right hand.

[58]

IX

Observations to Facilitate Accompaniment in the Natural and Transposed Modes

All the natural notes have their natural intervals on natural keys, except *Fa*, whose fourth is played on *Si* flat, and *Si*, whose fifth is played on *Fa* sharp.

All the sharped and flatted notes have their fourth, fifth and octave on accidentals except *Fa* sharp, whose fourth is *Si* natural, and *Si* flat, whose fifth is *Fa* natural.

The notes of the natural chords of *Re* sharp and *La* sharp are all taken on accidentals.

All intervals which are not natural to natural notes are taken on accidentals.[248] Thus, [augmented and diminished] seconds, thirds, sixths, and sevenths are played on the accidental keys, as are tritones and diminished fifths, except for the tritone of *Fa* and the diminished fifth of *Si*, which are found on natural [keys] on the keyboard.

Intervals which are not natural to the notes that are naturally sharped and flatted [in a given key] are taken on accidental keys, together with their fifths and their octaves.

Tritones and diminished fifths above flatted or sharped notes are played on natural keys.

[59]

One will remark that the chords in the right hand must be taken at a suitable distance to the bass, proportionate to how much the bass ascends or descends. One should take the chords above the range of the

---

[248]i.e., augmented and diminished intervals above diatonic notes.

[bass] notes which follow, so as not to be obliged to raise the chords in the treble conjointly with the bass. [Raising the hands simultaneously] could not be done without encumbering the hands by putting them in too close a proximity, and without producing parallel fifths or octaves. Conversely, when the bass descends several notes, one should take the chords of the right hand as close to the bass as possible. One should have the freedom to ascend afterwards, if necessary, but should avoid too large an interval between the hands.

To facilitate practicing the position of the hands, whether the bass ascends or descends, [several rules should be followed]. When the bass ascends several notes, the right-hand chords should be taken more than an octave above the first note of the bass; with the left hand, one should fill in the gap between the two hands as much as possible. Always lower the chord tones played by the left hand in proportion to how much the bass ascends. For example, after playing the octave of the bass with the left hand on the first of several ascending notes in the bass, one would play only the fifth or the sixth on the following note, the third on the note after that, and, finally, only the bass, as one will see in the following example.

Ex. 211

If the bass ascends in such a way that one is obliged to raise the chords as well, this must be done by disengaging the right hand above a [bass] note which takes a sixth chord. Then, by omitting the octave and playing only the third and the sixth, doubled as much as one wishes, parallel fifths and octaves will be avoided.

When the bass descends a great deal, the chords in the right hand should be taken as close to the bass as possible. As the bass descends, one should fill in with the left hand the appropriate chord tones found in the space between the two hands.

[60]

Ex. 212

One may double all the notes of figured and unfigured chords, as long as they are not dissonances.

X

Rules for *Suppositions*[249]

The *supposition* is made when several notes of equal value follow one another, ascending or descending; only the second note of the beats of the measure carries [a chord], not the first.

It is impossible to give completely general rules to explain *suppositions*, since their use depends on the wishes of composers, and the same notes that can pass by means of *supposition* can also pass without *supposition*.

Suppositions are used to connect the tones of a melody. Ordinarily, they are made when the bass ascends by third or fourth, and then descends by one or several degrees (A,B,C,D). Only the first and last notes of these intervals carry a chord. It is the same when the bass descends by one or several degrees (E,F). *Suppositions* are also made when the bass descends several notes. Then, only the second note of each beat carries a chord (G).

On all *suppositions*, one plays, on the first note of the beat, the chords suitable to the second.

It would be desirable if one marked the *suppositions* by a slur to indicate what notes carry chords.[250]

---

[249]In this section, Delair describes the use of melodic *suppositions*, i.e., dissonant passing tones, which may be added to the bass with the justification that dissonances merely suppose, or substitute for, displaced consonances. In the "General Rules," Delair discusses the concept of harmonic *suppositions*, whereby dissonant intervals above the bass may be substituted for consonant ones provided they are properly prepared and resolved. Rameau's usage of this term to mean implied chord-root is unique.

[250]The notational reform proposed here by Delair does not seem to have gained wide acceptance by his peers.

In the following example, one will see the most usual *suppositions*; one can distinguish the notes which should carry a chord by the natural melody which I have put underneath the *suppositions*. This will clarify the preceding rules.

[61]

Ex. 213: *Suppositions*

Addendum (1724 Edition)

[62]

In the preliminaries of this treatise, I spoke of the keys and the modes in relation to *natural harmony*.[251] Besides this, one must also understand *extraordinary harmony*,[252] which, like *natural harmony*, consists of [playing] the principal and the leading tone appropriately on all successive notes encompassed by the octave. However, these notes, that is to say, the leading tone and the principal, are placed differently in each of these two harmonies since, in *extraordinary harmony*, one puts the leading tone in the place of the principal and the principal in the place of the leading tone.

Ex. 214

[63]

Extraordinary harmony differs from *natural harmony*--where the natural chord is played on the principal and the dominant, and the sixth is played on all the other notes of the octave--in that, *extraordinary harmony* consists in the use of false dissonances, namely, those that are augmented and diminished. This harmony is suitable only to the minor mode. To use it profitably and knowledgeably, note what [interval] the leading tone forms with all the notes of the octave. In the minor mode, the leading tone produces a major seventh on the principal note, a major sixth on the second, a major third on the dominant, and a tritone on the

---

[251]Diatonic harmony.
[252]Chromatic harmony.

fourth, like in the major mode. However, in minor, the leading tone
produces an augmented fifth on the mediant and an augmented second on
the sixth of the key.

[In the minor mode], the sixth of the key forms all the diminished
intervals. It makes a diminished fifth on the second degree of the key, a
minor third on the fourth or a diminished third when the fourth is
sharped, and a diminished seventh on the leading tone.

Extraordinary harmony consists of more than playing diminished
and augmented intervals; these are not [even] obtained or used in the
major mode, where the only false intervals are the tritone and the
diminished fifth. *Extraordinary harmony* consists, besides, in playing
extraordinary accompaniments, in which diminished intervals are
accompanied by major intervals, and augmented intervals by minor
intervals. These are obtained by playing the leading tone with the sixth
of the key. Although these two notes oppose one another--forming
between them the interval of an augmented second when the sixth is the
lower, or the diminished seventh when the leading tone is the lower--
they are nevertheless like two poles around which the whole key turns,
and together, they make a more complete harmony than when separated.

[64]

Ex. 215

[In the above example], one sees the *sixth of the key* played with
the leading tone on the principal, second, third, fourth and sixth degrees
of the key. The *sixth of the key* is also played on the leading tone; the
diminished seventh resulting is a more appropriate accompaniment than
the *sixth of the leading tone* would be.[253]

I know that the diminished third, which I have included among the
intervals in this treatise and which is indicated on *Sol* sharp at the end
of the preceding example, disgusts most accompanists, but this is
unfounded, since the rule of intervals and rule of modulation call for it.

One will agree that when the bass descends a major third, the major
third is played on the last note; similarly, when the bass descends a
minor third, the minor third is played. Thus, when the bass descends a
diminished third, the diminished third must be played on that note.

---

[253]In other words, Delair prefers to harmonize the seventh degree of the scale with
7b/5/3 instead of 6/5/3 in the minor mode.

One cannot abolish this principle with respect to the *rule of intervals*, which requires that when the bass descends a third, the third of the last note must be of the same species as the interval of the bass.

It is even more difficult to suppress this principle as it relates to the *rule of modulation*,[254] which requires that the sixth of the minor mode always be minor when it descends to the dominant. It can be sharped only when it ascends to the leading tone. This is how organists, none of whom are in the least troubled [by their error], avoid [playing the diminished third]. However, those who accompany, being bound to the figures, must conform to them. Consequently, they must descend to the dominant when the fourth is marked on the dominant; this cannot be done, except by semitone, without going against the rules of intervals and of modulation.

[65]

It should be observed that it is not the [flatted] sixth--an essential pitch of the minor mode--that shocks the ear, but rather the fourth of the key, which lies outside the mode by a sharp and therefore is not appropriate. If one sharped the sixth instead, there would not be one pitch that did not clash with the mode. Thus, it is more suitable, for the reasons stated above, to play the diminished rather than the sharped third.

It must be noted, moreover, that melodic intervals may become harmonic intervals. Consequently, since the interval of a diminished third is very frequent [in melodic progressions], one can make a harmonic interval with it. If the diminished third is not used at all, that is but a vice of education, which arises because writers do not include it among the number of available intervals. However, one should use it for the above reasons, which are incontestable.

It is not enough to understand the concepts of key, mode, modulation, natural harmony, extraordinary harmony and extraordinary accompaniments. Besides this, one must know *harmony by interval*, which consists in the use of just dissonances. These are the second, the fourth, the seventh and the ninth. This harmony is the foundation of sonatas, in which one sees these dissonances on almost every note. Natural harmony is the foundation of operas, in which one sees almost nothing but the natural chord and sixths, especially in the operas of M[r]. de Lully.

A difference between the just and false dissonances is that the latter do not have to be prepared by syncopation or conjunct degree; it is enough that they be resolved. The diminished intervals descend by a degree, and the augmented ascend by a degree.

Another difference is that false dissonances (augmented or diminished intervals) are not played without the addition of a flat or a

---

[254]The term *modulation* refers to the progression of tones and semitones within the octave.

sharp. The just dissonances, on the other hand, do not require a flat or a sharp.

[66]

Harmony by interval contrasts with *natural* and *extraordinary harmony*, which conserve the key by the transposition of the leading tone and the principal. *Harmony by interval*, on the other hand, consists of a progression of dissonances which follow one another, being prepared and resolved in turn by the notes that enter into their accompaniments. These progressions have no fixed key, in that the leading tone plays no part in them, since it does not enter into each [chord] with the principal, as in the above-mentioned harmonies. This will be observed in the progressions of dissonances which we will discuss.

A progression of second chords is obtained when the bass descends by several syncopated notes in conjunct motion. One plays a 6/5/3 chord or 3-4-5 on the first part of the note which follows that on which one played the second. One may play the minor second in a progression of seconds when the mode requires it.

Ex. 216

Progressions of fourths resolved by thirds are obtained when the bass descends a fourth and ascends afterwards a fifth, and when several of these intervals follow one another.

Ex. 217

Progressions of fourths resolved by octaves are obtained on the same intervals of an ascending fifth and a descending fourth, but the bass must ascend a third between these intervals.

Ex. 218

Progressions of fourths resolved by thirds, alternating with ninths resolved by octaves, are played when the bass descends a fourth and ascends a degree several times in succession.

Ex. 219

[67]

Fourths resolved by octaves, and ninths resolved by sixths, are played on the same intervals as above, but the bass should ascend a third between these intervals.

Ex. 220

One can also play progressions of fourths on a bass that ascends by conjunct degree, but one must disengage the right hand at the end of each note, [playing] the fifth [of the chord in the top voice] in order to prepare the fourth above the following [bass] note.

Ex. 221

When the bass ascends several notes by conjunct degree, if one is not restricted to natural harmony and if the tempo is somewhat slow, [instead of] playing fifths and sixths in succession, one should play the seventh and ninth where the fifth is marked, and an 8/6/3 chord next, with the third on top.

Ex. 222

However, if the tempo is fast, only the third and the sixth are played.

Ex. 223

[68]

When the bass ascends from the principal to the dominant by conjunct degree, one plays the fourth and ninth resolved by the third and the octave on the second note; the ninth and the seventh resolved by the octave and the sixth on the third note; the seventh resolved by the sixth, on the fourth note; and the fourth resolved by the third on the fifth note.

Ex. 224

When the bass ascends four notes, one ordinarily plays the seventh on the second note.

Ex. 225

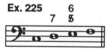

When the bass ascends four conjunct notes, descends a third, and then climbs four notes again, one plays the seventh and ninth on the second note, the seventh on the third note, and the natural chord on the last.

Ex. 226

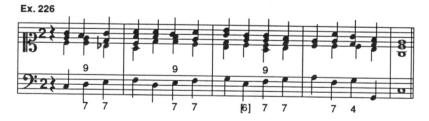

When the bass descends chromatically, one plays diminished fifths accompanied by sevenths followed by tritones. This is only done in the minor mode.

One can also play a seventh and a 6/4/3 chord successively above this chromatic progression. [This accompaniment is also appropriate for progressions in which] the bass descends several diatonic notes by conjunct degree.

When the bass ascends a fourth and then descends a fifth, a seventh is played on all the notes.

Above these same [bass] intervals of an ascending fourth and a descending fifth, one can play minor sevenths accompanied by major thirds.

When the bass ascends a degree and then descends a third, the ninth is played on the second [bass] note, and a fifth and sixth on the third note.

Here are the principal chord progressions in use. One must work diligently at learning the different intervals [of the bass] to which they are appropriate in order to play them at the right moment.

I have only notated the simple [bass] melody of the chord progressions. Once the [bass] notes are figured, it will be easy to distinguish those which should carry [chords] from those that are put between them [as ornamental tones]. To differentiate between them, one merely need notice which notes begin each beat.

The *point d'orgue* is the last topic remaining to be discussed.

A note of the bass on which one plays different chords is called a *point d'orgue*.

Points *d'orgue* can be made on the principal or on the dominant; with the majority being on the dominant. They ordinarily consist of two chords that follow one another, namely, those of the fourth and major third. Observe that one plays the sixth and the octave with the fourth, and the minor seventh and the fifth with the third. After playing this seventh, one descends by conjunct degree to the third, after which one ascends again by step to the octave, continuing to descend and to ascend as long as the *point d'orgue* lasts.

Ex. 232

The *point d'orgue* can also be made on the principal. It ordinarily consists of two alternating chords, that is, the natural chord and the major seventh, accompanied by the second and the fourth. The chords in the right hand should descend by conjunct degree from the fifth to the seventh, and then ascend by the same degrees to the fifth.

Ex. 233

There are also other *points d'orgue* which consist of a series of dissonances made between the parts. They ordinarily form the interval of a second between themselves, and are resolved successively by conjunct degree. One is guided in this by the figures or by the parts.

Ex. 234

After acquiring a knowledge of the dissonant progressions, it is very useful to know the [bass] intervals on which one can play dissonances, even if they are not figured. Concerning this, one will observe that when the bass ascends a semitone, if a diminished fifth is played on the first note, the fourth and the ninth are prepared and thus can be played either together or separately, as long as the parts do not clash. For example, if there were a third in [one of] the parts, one could play the ninth, but not the fourth.

Ex. 235

When the bass ascends a tone, and a natural chord is played on the first note, the fourth, the seventh and the ninth may be played, together or separately.

Ex. 236

When the bass ascends a third, no dissonance is prepared (A), unless a sixth is played on the first note, which prepares the fourth (B) [on the second note].

Ex. 237

When the bass ascends a fourth or descends a fifth, the seventh and the ninth are prepared.

When the bass ascends a fifth or descends a fourth, the only dissonance that can be played is the fourth.

[71]

When the bass ascends a sixth or descends a third, only the seventh can be played.

When the bass descends a tone, and if a 6/4/3 is played on the first note, the fourth and the seventh are prepared. They may be played together if the sixth is minor (A), but if the sixth is major, only the fourth can be played on the second note (B).

Those skilled in the art do not overlook the possibility of playing dissonances that have been prepared, even if they are not figured, as long as nothing [in the accompaniment] clashes with the parts, and provided that the dissonances can be resolved. It is not sufficient to know where one can play dissonances. Since one should not play them unless they can be resolved, it is also necessary to know all the ways in which one can resolve them. One is frequently obliged to accompany unfigured basses, over which one could thoughtlessly play a dissonance that has been prepared, but that cannot be resolved, and this would be worth nothing. One will learn how each dissonance may be resolved.

There is [little] to be said about the second, which is resolved by the bass, since it is the bass which is a syncopation and, consequently, must descend by a degree. Unless the bass is syncopated, the second should not be played, as was seen in the example of the progression of seconds.

The syncopation of a fourth is resolved by the third (A), the tritone (B), the diminished fifth (C), the major sixth (D) and the octave (E).

Ex. 242

[72]

The seventh is resolved by the third (A), the fifth (B), the diminished fifth (C), the augmented fifth (D), the sixth (E), the seventh (F), the octave (G), the tritone (H) and the consonant fourth (I).

Ex. 243

The ninth is resolved by the octave (A), the third (B), the sixth (C), the fifth (D) and the diminished fifth (E).

Ex. 244

Herein are contained the most commonly used and learned [principles] concerning *harmony by interval*. Those who master the preceding rules will know how to make up for the defect of omitted figures, and will accompany without inconsistency and with the utmost perfection when using *natural harmony*. To accompany using *extraordinary harmony*, all that is required is a knowledge of the *rule of the octave*. One merely has to observe what [harmonies] the leading tone and the sixth of the key produce on each note of the octave, and to practice false dissonances, that is, augmented and diminished intervals. While more could have been said about *harmony by interval*, which is the principal foundation of accompaniment, I think nothing has been omitted that is necessary to a knowledge of this harmony.

Bibliography

Seventeenth- and Eighteenth-Century Sources

Anglebert, Jean-Henry d'. *Pièces de clavecin . . . avec la manière de les jouer . . . et les principes de l'accompagnement*. Paris: l'autheur, 1689. Facs. ed., New York: Broude, 1965. Modern ed. Kenneth Gilbert, Paris: Heugel, 1975.

Bach, Carl Philipp Emanuel. *Versuch Über die wahre Art, das Clavier zu spielen*. Berlin: 1759. Trans. William Mitchell as *Essay on the True Art of Playing Keyboard Instruments*. New York: Norton, 1949.

Bacilly, Bénigne de. *Remarques curieuses sur l'art de bien chanter*. Paris: Ballard et l'auteur, 1668. Facs. of 1679 reprint ed. Geneva: Minkoff, 1971. Trans. Austin B. Caswell as *A Commentary on the Art of Proper Singing*. Brooklyn: Institute of Medieval Music, 1968.

Bartolotti (Bartolomi), Angelo Michele. *Table pour apprendre à toucher le théorbe sur la basse continue*. Paris: Ballard, 1669.

Boyvin, Jacques. "Traité abrégé d'accompagnement pour l'orgue et pour le clavessin," *Second livre d'orgue*. Paris: Ballard, 1700; ed. Guilmant and Pirro, Archives des maîtres de l'orgue, vol. 8. Paris: Eschig, 1940, pp. 74-87.

Brossard, Sebastian de. *Dictionnaire de musique contenant une explication des termes grecs, latins, italiens, & françois les plus usitez dans la musique*. Paris: Christophe Ballard, 1703. Facs. ed. Amsterdam: Antigua, 1964.

Campion, François. *Traité d'accompagnement et de composition selon la règle des octaves de musique*. Paris: Amsterdam, 1716. Facs. ed. Geneva: Minkoff, 1976.

--------*Addition au traité d'accompagnement par la règle de l'octave.* Paris: Ribou, Boivin, Le Clerc, et l'auteur, 1730. Facs. ed. Geneva: Minkoff, 1976.

Charpentier, Marc-Antoine. "*Règles de composition.*" Paris: MS, c. 1692. Facs. and English ed. by L.M. Ruff, *The Consort*, vol. 24 (1967), pp. 233-270.

Chaumont, Lambert. "Petit traité de l'accompagnement." *Pièces d'orgue sur les huit tons.* Liège: Danielis, 1695. Ed. Paris: Heugel, 1970.

Choron, Alexandre and Fayolle, François. *Dictionnaire historique des musiciens.* Paris: Chez Valade et Lenormant, 1810, s.v. "Delair (D.)" and "Delaire."

Corrette, Michel. *Le maître de clavecin pour l'accompagnement.* Paris, 1753. Later edns. 1755 (?), 1790. Facs. ed. Bologna: Forni, 1970.

Couperin, François. "Règles pour l'accompagnement" (c. 1698). Ed. M. Cauchie, *Oeuvres complètes*, vol. I. Paris: l'Oiseau lyre, 1933, pp. 13-17.

Dandrieu, Jean-François. *Principes de l'accompagnement du clavecin.* Paris, 1719. Facs. ed. Geneva: Minkoff, 1972.

Delair, Denis. *Traité d'accompagnement pour le théorbe, et le clavecin.* Paris: l'auteur, 1690. Facs. ed. Geneva: Minkoff, 1972.

--------*Nouveau traité d'accompagnement.* Paris: l'auteur, 1724.

DeLaPorte, Claude. *Traité théorique et pratique de l'accompagnement.* Paris: l'auteur, Boivin and Leclerc, 1753. Facs. ed. Geneva: Minkoff, 1972.

Denis, Jean. *Traité de l'accord de l'espinette.* Paris: Ballard, 1650. Facs. ed. New York: Da Capo, 1969.

Dubugrarre, M^r. *Méthode plus courte et plus facile que l'ancienne pour l'accompagnement du clavecin.* Paris: l'auteur, 1754. Facs. ed. Geneva: Minkoff, 1972.

Du Pradel, N. de Blégny, dit Abraham. *Le livre commode des addresses de Paris.* Paris, 1691, 1692; printed in Marcelle Benoit, *Versailles et les musiciens du roi: 1660-1733; étude institutionelle et sociale.* Paris: Editions A.& J. Picard, 1971, Annexe III, p. 413.

Fleury, Nicolas. *Méthode pour apprendre facilement à toucher le théorbe sur la basse continue.* Paris: Ballard, 1660. Facs. ed. Geneva: Minkoff, 1972.

Freillon-Poncein, Jean-Pierre. *La véritable manière d'apprendre à jouer en perfection du hautbois, de la flûte, et du flageolet.* Paris: Collombat, 1700. Facs. ed. Geneva: Minkoff, 1974.

Furetière, Antoine. *Dictionnaire universel, contenant généralement tous les mot françois tant vieux que modernes, & les termes des sciences et des arts.* 2 vols. The Hague & Rotterdam: A.& R. Leers, 1690.

Gasparini, Francesco. *l'Armonico practico al cimbalo*. Venice, 1708. Later edns. Venice, 1715, 1729, 1745, 1764, 1802, and Bologna, 1713, 1722. Trans. by Frank S. Stillings as *The Practical Harmonist at the Harpsichord*. New Haven: Music Theory Translation Series, 1963.

Grenerin, Henry. *Livre de théorbe*. Paris: l'autheur, ca. 1682. Facs. ed. Geneva: Minkoff, 1984.

Hotteterre, Jacques. *L'art de préluder sur la flûte traversière*. Paris: l'auteur, 1719. Facs. ed Geneva: Minkoff, 1978.

[Journal de Trévoux], 1732, *Mémoires pour l'histoire des sciences et des beaux arts*. Issue of January, 1732, vol. 122. Facs. ed. Geneva: Slatkine Reprints, 1968.

L'Affilard, Michel. *Principes très faciles pour bien apprendre la musique*. Paris: Ballard, 1705. Facs. ed. Geneva: Minkoff, 1976.

Loulié, Etienne. *Elémens ou principes de musique mis dans un nouvel ordre*. Paris: Ballard et l'auteur, 1696. Trans. and ed. Albert Cohen in *Musical Theorists in Translation*, vol. 6. New York: Institute of Mediaeval Music, 1965.

La Viéville de Freneuse, Jean-Laurent Le Cerf de. *Comparaison de la musique italienne et de la musique françoise*. 4 vols. Brussels: 1704-1706. Reprinted in Bourdelot's *Histoire de la Musique*, 1715, later edns. 1721, 1725, 1726, 1743.

La Voye Mignot, de. *Traité de la musique*. Paris: Ballard, 1656. Trans. Albion Gruber in *Musical Theorists in Translation*, vol. 11. New York: Institute of Mediaeval Music, 1972.

Masson, Charles. *Nouveau traité des règles pour la composition de la musique*. Paris: Ballard, 1694. Facs. of 1699 with an intro. by Imogene Horseley. New York: Da Capo Press, 1967.

Mersenne, Marin. *Correspondence du P. Marin Mersenne*, ed. Cornelius de Waard. Paris: Presses Universitaires de France, 1945.

--------*Harmonie universelle*. Paris: 1636. Facs. ed. Paris: Éditions du centre national pour la recherche scientifique, 1975. Vol. III translated by Roger E. Chapman as *Harmonie universelle: The Books on Instruments*. The Hague: Martinus Nijhoff, 1957.

Meude-Monpas, J.J.O. *Dictionnaire de musique*. Paris: chez Knapen et Fils, 1787. Facs. ed. Geneva: Minkoff, 1981.

Nivers, Guillaume-Gabriel. *Motets à voix seule . . . avec l'art d'accompagner sur la basse continue pour l'orgue et le clavecin*. Paris: l'auteur, 1689, pp. 149-170.

Ouvrard, René. *Secret pour composer en musique*. Paris: 1658.

Ozanam, Jacques. *Dictionnaire mathématique*. Paris: Michallet, 1691 (and later edns.), s.v. *Musique*, pp. 640-672.

Penna, Lorenzo. *Li prima albori musicali*. Bologna, 1672. Facs. of 1684 reprint. Bologna: Forni Editions, 1969.

Rameau, Jean-Philippe. *Traité de l'harmonie réduite à ses principes naturels.* Paris: Ballard, 1722. Trans. Philip Gossett as *Treatise on Harmony.* New York: Dover, 1971.

--------*Dissertation sur les différentes méthodes d'accompagnement pour le clavecin, ou pour l'orgue.* Paris: Boivin & Le Clair, 1732.

Rousseau, Jean. *Méthode claire, certaine et facile pour apprendre à chanter la musique,* 4th ed. Amsterdam: Estienne Roger, 1691; 5th ed. Amsterdam, c. 1720. Facs. of 1710 ed. Geneva: Minkoff, 1976.

--------*Traité de la viole.* Paris: Ballard, 1687. Trans. by Robert Green as *Annotated Translation and Commentary on the Works of J. Rousseau: A Study of Late Seventeenth-Century Musical Thought and Performance Practice,* Ph.D. Diss., Indiana University, 1979. Ann Arbor: University Microfilms, 1980.

Rousseau, Jean-Jacques. *Dictionnaire de musique.* Paris: Duchesne, 1768. Reprint ed. New York: AMS Press, 1975.

Saint Lambert, M. de. *Nouveau traité de l'accompagnement du clavecin et de l'orgue.* Paris: Ballard, 1707. Facs. ed. Geneva: Minkoff, 1974. Later edn. Amsterdam: Roger, c. 1710. Trans. James Burchill as Saint Lambert's *Nouveau traité de l'accompagnement: a Translation and Commentary,* Ph.D. Diss., University of Rochester, 1979. Ann Arbor: University Microfilms, 1979. Trans. by John Powell as *A New Treatise on Accompaniment.* Bloomington: Indiana University Press, 1991.

--------*Principes du clavecin.* Paris: Ballard, 1702. Facs. ed. Geneva; Minkoff, 1974. Trans. as *Principles of the Harpsichord by Monsieur de Saint Lambert* by Rebecca Harris-Warrick. Cambridge: Cambridge University Press, 1984.

Nineteenth and Twentieth-Century Sources

Anderson, Gene Henry. *Musical Terminology in J.P. Rameau's "Traité de l'harmonie": A Study and Glossary Based on an Index.* Ph.D. Dissertation, University of Iowa, 1981. Ann Arbor: University Microfilms, 1984.

Arnold, Frank Thomas. *The Art of Accompaniment from a Thoroughbass.* London: Oxford University Press, 1931. Reprint ed. New York: Dover, 1965.

Atcherson, Walter. "Key and Mode in Seventeenth-Century Music Theory Books." *Journal of Music Theory,* vol. 172 (Fall, 1973), pp. 204-232.

Bates, Robert. *From Mode to Key: a Study of 17th-century French Liturgical Organ Music and Music Theory.* Ph.D. Dissertation, Stanford University, 1986.

Boalch, Donald H. *Makers of the Harpsichord and Clavichord 1440-1840*. Oxford: Clarendon Press, 1974.

Buelow, George J. "The Full-voiced Style of Thorough-Bass Realization." *Acta Musicologica*, vol. 35 (1963), p. 159.

--------*Thorough-Bass Accompaniment According to Johann David Heinichen*. Berkeley and Los Angeles: University of California Press, 1966

Cohen, Albert. "*La supposition* and the Changing Concept of Dissonance in Baroque Theory." *Journal of the American Musicological Society*, vol. 24 (1971), pp. 63-84.

Dictionnaire de Biographie Française, direction Roman d'Amat. Paris VI: Librairie Letouzy et Ané, 1975, vol. 13.

Fétis, François J. *Biographie universelle des musiciens et bibliographie générale de la musique*. 2nd ed. Paris: Firmin Didot Frères, 1866-70.

Gallet, Babelon. *Demeures parisiennes, l'époque de Louis XVI*. Paris: 1964.

Garros, Madeleine. "L'art d'accompagner sur la basse continue d'après Guillaume-Gabriel Nivers." *Mélanges d'Histoire et d'Esthétique Musicales*, ed. Masson, vol. 2. Paris: Richard-Masse, 1955, pp. 45-51.

Gruber, Albion. *Evolving Tonal Theory in Seventeenth-Century France*. Ph.D. Dissertation, University of Rochester, 1969.

Houle, George. *Meter in Music, 1600-1800*. Bloomington: Indiana University Press, 1987.

Hubbard, Frank. *Three Centuries of Harpsichord Making*. Cambridge: Harvard University Press, 1967.

La Laurencie, L. de la. "Un musicien piémontais en France au XVIIIe siècle: J.P. Guignon, dernier *Roy des violons*." *Rivista Musicale Italiana*, vol. 18 (1911), p. 711.

Lindley, Mark. *Lutes, Viols and Temperaments*. Cambridge: Cambridge University Press, 1984.

Mason, Kevin. "François Campion's *Secret of Accompaniment for the Theorbo, Guitar and Lute*." *Lute Society of America Journal*, vol. 14 (1981), pp. 69-94.

Mather, Betty Bang. *Dance Rhythms of the French Baroque: A Handbook for Performance*. Bloomington: Indiana University Press, 1987.

Mangsen, Sandra. "The Unfigured Bass and the Continuo Player: More Evidence from France." *Early Keyboard Journal*. Southeastern Historical Keyboard Society, vol. 3 (1984-85), pp. 5-12.

North, Nigel. *Continuo Playing on the Lute, Archlute and Theorbo*. Bloomington: Indiana University Press, 1987.

Pardailhé-Galabrun, Annik. *La Naissance de l'Intime: 3000 foyers parisiens XVIIe-XVIIIe siècles.* Paris: Presses Universitaires de France, 1988.

Pesce, Dolores. *The Affinities and Medieval Transposition.* Bloomington: Indiana University Press, 1987.

Pruitt, William. "The Organ Works of G.-G. Nivers (1631-1714)." *Recherches sur la musique française classique,* vol. 14 (1974), pp. 38-42.

Quittard, Henri. "Le théorbe comme instrument d'accompagnement." *Bulletin français de la société internationale de musique,* vol. 6 (1910), pp. 231-237.

Russell, Raymond. *The Harpsichord and Clavichord,* 2nd ed. New York: W. W. Norton & Company, Inc., 1973.

Sadie, Stanley, ed. *The New Grove Dictionary of Music and Musicians,* 20 vols. Washington, D.C.: Grove's Dictionaries of Music, 1980.

Williams, Peter. *Figured Bass Accompaniment.* Edinburgh: Edinburgh University Press, 1970, 1977.

--------"The Harpsichord Acciaccatura: Theory and Practice in Harmony 1650-1750." *Musical Quarterly* 54/4 (October, 1968), pp. 503-23.

Zenatti, Arlette. "La Prélude dans la musique profane de clavier en France au XVIIIe siècle." *Recherches sur la musique française classique,* vol. 5 (1965), p. 179.

Index